"This book opens up new analytic ground for grappling with some of the most difficult and complex issues of our time. And it gives us pragmatic answers that can take us out of the spirals of current strategy. Westbrook avoids familiar tropes and gives us an original point of view. A great book that should be widely read."
—*Saskia Sassen, Professor of Sociology and Co-Chair, Committee on Global Thought, Columbia University*

"Excellent. . . . Westbrook is refreshingly direct and realistic. He cuts through so much of the cant surrounding the global war on terror."
—*Andrew Bacevich, Professor of History and International Relations at Boston University and author of* The Limits of Power

"Highly readable, *Deploying Ourselves* builds a persuasive case for extending the classical political framework for the legitimate use of military force to the global polity, leading to sound advice for conducting the war against terrorists. It should be read by concerned citizens as well as responsible government officials."
—*Lt. General (USA, Ret.) Robert G. Gard, Jr., Ph.D.*

"This timely book by David Westbrook makes a powerful case for understanding the U.S. war against Muslim extremism as also and ultimately a political battle for Muslim hearts and minds. His unconventional but persuasive argument, inspired not by sympathy for Islam or the Muslim world but by a realistic rethinking of the arts of both war and statecraft in a global age, should prove a useful counterweight to current tendencies to short-circuit the cultural and diplomatic, not just military, tasks before us."
—*Frank Vogel, Director of the Islamic Legal Studies Program at Harvard Law School*

"This thought-provoking book reflects on the need to re-examine security policy in an increasingly interdependent world, where threats to peace have taken new and ever more dangerous forms. As Westbrook points out, we cannot expect strategies designed for other times and other types of enemies to be optimal for addressing the conflicts that have arisen in our globalized age. Moving well beyond debates over "hard" and "soft" power, and disdaining partisan politics, he offers practical suggestions for a security policy that is smarter about politics in the classical sense of ordering our lives together. *Deploying Ourselves* is a timely, important work that deserves to be widely discussed."

> —*Mary Ann Glendon, Learned Hand Professor of Law,*
> *Harvard University, and former U.S. Ambassador to the Holy See*

"With the rhetorical power and texture of Tom Paine's *Common Sense*, this gripping work of deep intellect, diagnostic acumen, and stunning turns of phrase leads to proposals of reform in the conduct of our foreign, military, and security/intelligence affairs that make radical common sense."

> —*George E. Marcus, Chancellor's Professor of Anthropology,*
> *University of California at Irvine, and Member of the American*
> *Anthropology Association's Commission on the Engagement of*
> *Anthropology with the U.S. Security and Intelligence Communities*

DEPLOYING OURSELVES

NEW
WORLDS
S E R I E S

A New Series from Paradigm Publishers
Edited by Charles Lemert

FORTHCOMING TITLES

On Time and the World-System, Immanuel Wallerstein

America 3,000, Charles Lemert

Black Men: How Does It Feel to be a "Problem," Al Young

Cities, Raymond Joshua Scannell

Virtual Epidemics, Monica Achitoff Gray

DEPLOYING OURSELVES

Islamist Violence and the
Responsible Projection of U.S. Force

DAVID A. WESTBROOK

Paradigm Publishers

Boulder • London

Copyright © 2011 by Paradigm Publishers

Published in the United States by Paradigm Publishers, 2845 Wilderness Place, Suite 200, Boulder, Colorado 80301 USA.

Paradigm Publishers is the trade name of Birkenkamp & Company, LLC, Dean Birkenkamp, President and Publisher.

Library of Congress Cataloging-in-Publication Data

Westbrook, David A.
    Deploying ourselves : Islamist violence and the responsible projection of U.S. force / David A. Westbrook.
        p.   cm. — (New world series)
    Includes bibliographical references and index.
    ISBN 978-1-59451-743-3 (hc : alk. paper) — ISBN 978-1-59451-744-0 (pbk : alk. paper)
    1. United States — Foreign relations—21st century. 2. United States — Military policy. 3. National security--United States. 4. Intelligence service — United States. 5. Islamic fundamentalism--Government policy — United States. 6. Terrorism — Government policy — United States. I. Title.
    JZ1480.W47 2011
    327.1'170973—dc22   2010033661

Printed and bound in the United States of America on acid-free paper that meets the standards of the American National Standard for Permanence of Paper for Printed Library Materials.

15 14 13 12 11   5 4 3 2 1

Nations, like individuals, are punished for their transgressions.

—ULYSSES S. GRANT[1]

CONTENTS

ACKNOWLEDGMENTS

I have worked on this book for many years now and owe thanks to a few institutions and to many people. Even though a number of individuals contributed to this effort in more than one way, for the sake of clarity, these generous souls are thanked only once here.

Some of this book has been published before, and therefore copyright issues and simple provenance ought to be recognized. Although rewriting, revision, and so forth has been substantial, traces of earlier publication may remain. Insofar as this book replicates texts previously published elsewhere, republication is by permission, which is gratefully acknowledged.

In May of 2010, I gave a program of talks throughout Pakistan as part of the U.S. State Department's U.S. Speakers Program. My visit concerned possibilities for economic development, which in Pakistan are inextricably bound up with security issues. I learned a great deal from the foreign service officers and from the many Pakistanis that I had the opportunity to meet. I thank the State Department, and especially Barbara Durant in Washington, and the many foreign service officers and local employees of the State Department in Pakistan who made my visit possible.

Many of the ideas in this book were presented in two talks to security analysts at NATO's Supreme Headquarters Allied Powers Europe (SHAPE), outside Mons, Belgium, in November of 2006 and March of 2008. I also learned a great deal from the analysts there, and I thank them.

Parts of Chapters Three, Six, Eight, Nine, and Eleven appeared first in "Bin Laden's War," a long essay published by the *Buffalo Law Review*. A more policy-oriented version of these ideas, with more attention to the strategic consequences of the analysis, was published in *Orbis*.

Much of Chapter Six, "Politics Is Now," was delivered as a talk, "The Time of Faith: Contemporary Muslims, Secularists, and Anxieties over the Nature of History," at the conference "Does Islam Need a Reformulation to be Compatible with the West?" at Columbia University, March 29, 2006, sponsored by the Alliance Program (Columbia University; Ecole Polytechnique; Sciences Po; Universite Paris 1 Pantheon Sorbonne) and the Middle East Institute of Columbia University's School of International and Public Affairs (SIPA).

Some of the thinking in Chapters Seven and Eleven was presented, albeit in substantially different form, as "Holding Positions in a Time of Targeted Killing" at a studio conference given by the University of California Institute for Humanities Research and the Center for Ethnography at the University of California, Irvine.

Much of the book's thinking on the multiplicity of our conceptions of what it means to be "modern" was originally presented as "Theorizing the Diffusion of Law: Conceptual Difficulties, Unstable Imaginations, and the Effort to Think Gracefully Nonetheless," the keynote address to the symposium "The Diffusion of Law in the Twenty-First Century," Harvard Law School, March 4, 2006, and published in the *Harvard International Law Journal*.

Turning from acknowledging institutions to thanking individuals, this book brings together a great deal of learning, and more precious still, considered judgments, attained by others. I have been blessed with conversations, and I hope my interlocutors approve of the uses to which I put their hard-earned truths.

With regard to matters Islamic, many people have deepened my thought, including Amel Boubekeur, Michael Fischer, Mohamed Ramdane, and Richard Whelan. Frank Vogel taught me whatever sensitivity I have to Islamic law. Exchanges with both Frank and Olivier Roy have helped me think about the contemporary cultural situations of Muslims and have encouraged me at key junctures. And this rather audacious project could not have been completed without the support and particularly enthusiasm of Vincent Littrell, a quality even more appreciated than his nearly encyclopedic knowledge and thoughtful perspective. I am thankful to all.

As will become clear, this book is an intensely patriotic, and I hope constructive, yet fundamental critique of the nation's security policy and particularly institutions. In my efforts to understand and seriously address such questions, I have benefited from conversations with many people now or formerly in the security community, and who, in some cases, read substantial amounts or even all of the text. Specifically, I owe debts to Andrew Bacevich, Bill Casebeer, Robert Gard, Bob Gibbs, Michael Glennon, Laura McNamara, Miles Seeley, and Michael Sullivan.

Over the years, I have been helped by numerous research assistants on the book and on the various texts that the book incorporates. I thank Caroline Bancatella, Brian Carr, Khurram Khan, Ryk Perry, and Heidi Spalholz. The UB Library, and especially Lucy Olejnikova, did a wonderful job fulfilling my, usually harried, requests for often-arcane texts. Barb Kennedy helped with many texts and then Sarah Cranganu helped get the book out the door. The book as a whole owes a lot to majordomo Mike Halliday.

At various points and in sundry ways, a number of people gave me the nerve to carry on this campaign. I am not convinced that Quixote owes thanks, but Pierre d'Argent, Ermelinda Bonaccio, David Brent, John Eipper, Mary Ann Glendon, Keith Frome, Douglas Holmes, James Kurth, George Marcus, Marc Miller, and Craig Watson all offered advice and encouragement, listened to me struggle to weave disparate thoughts together, and said nice things at appropriate moments, however they might have felt about my obsession. Dean Birkenkamp and Charles Lemert have shown an appetite for risk befitting truly serious publishers, and I thank them for their trust in me. Jack Schlegel and my mother, Viola Westbrook, read the manuscript, and commented in ways I appreciate. And though she almost never wants to talk about "the war book," yet again and as always, I am grateful to Amy for protecting me.

I apologize to anyone that I should have thanked here, but have inadvertently overlooked.

As this book goes to press, the wars that occasioned its writing continue. There is too much more to say about what has already happened and is still happening. But politics does not wait, cannot wait, on history, much less the circumstances of a writer. This is what I could get done; it will have to serve as best it can. The failings are my own.

I dedicate this book to my father.

PART ONE

INTRODUCTION

CHAPTER ONE

LOOKING OUTWARD

Military Force as Political Speech

OVERVIEW

This book makes a fundamental claim and husbands a great hope.

The claim is that *politics, and hence an ethos of responsibility, can be used to judge, and so discipline, our exercise of military power.*

The hope is that *a politically responsible security policy will be more successful in the world, and in particular in the fight against Islamist violence, than our current efforts are.* The hope emerges, or does not, in the course of the book.

UNDERSTANDING FORCE IN POLITICAL TERMS

To deploy is to adopt some fighting posture toward an enemy and so before the world. If we citizens of the United States believe that we constitute a republican democracy in which the armed forces serve the national interest, then we are obliged to ask the question in explicitly political terms: How should we begin to think about our wars, and more generally, about the violence and threats of violence that are delivered in our name? How should we think about security policy, the web of people, institutions, and decisions that makes such violence possible, and that so variously affects how we in the United States, and indeed billions of other people, live? This book discusses certain strategic difficulties, moral temptations, and institutional possibilities for the United States as it deploys against what we commonly and roughly understand as Islamist violence, including the wars in Afghanistan and Iraq; worries over Indonesia, Pakistan, Iran, Yemen, Syria, Egypt, and Sudan and the rest of North Africa; Israel's wars always; homegrown extremism in the United States and Europe; and so forth.

In trying to think about how we voting Americans should deploy the forces we have available to us, I begin from Clausewitz's idea, so often repeated that it has become difficult to hear, that war is a form of politics. "When whole communities go to war—whole peoples, especially *civilized* peoples—the reason always lies in some political situation, and the occasion is always due to some political object. War, therefore, is an act of policy."[1] So what kind of wars, and more broadly, what kind of security policy, are appropriate expressions and causes of the politics that we as a nation wish to see in the world, even at the pain of violence? Despite the fact that Clausewitz has become a cliché, in the United States, security policy is neither designed nor often conducted as a political expression in any serious sense.

As of this writing, it is now widely recognized—or more precisely, it is said without objection—that the wars in Afghanistan and Iraq require counterinsurgency, and more broadly, are contests that must be won politically, not kinetically. Over the last couple of years, there has been a real turn in the nation's military institutions toward "culture," toward language (and law) training, toward recognition that establishing order matters. While this development is welcome if badly belated, it is unclear how deeply this new consensus runs. Especially in response to talk of a renewed commitment to Afghanistan, there is also much talk at present of killing terrorists by remote control; there is dissatisfaction with the rules of engagement ("ROE"); purchases of drones and other instruments for fighting without personal presence are up; and budgeting for intelligence services, many of them secret, has been increased. It is far from clear that we as a nation even know how to be serious, consequential, in our talk about the necessity of understanding these wars in political terms. And if we are serious about understanding our operations in political terms (as does classic counterinsurgency doctrine), it is not at all clear that our political aims will be achievable by the methods of counterinsurgency, that is, the large-scale human investment in a given country, perhaps Afghanistan—but that is the right question.

At least to date, counterinsurgency doctrine has been contested, and in some instances implemented, at the tactical and operational levels. While counterinsurgency, or COIN, is vitally important, it is not enough. In particular, the Obama administration's welcome internment of the Bush administration's phrase "Global War on Terror" (inevitably, given the military's fondness for acronyms, GWOT) risks an odd and wrongheaded renationalization of our security situation. It is true that the war in Afghanistan is not the war in Iraq and that al-Qaeda is not the Taliban. But it is more importantly also true that these conflicts happen within a Muslim, and global, context. Therefore, our approach to these conflicts should recognize that our violence is significant not just in the village or the valley, not just across the theater of operations, but around the world. We need to fight in full and awful recognition that how we fight establishes no small part of our nation's place in history and who we ultimately will be deemed to be—the stakes are constitutional and historical.

There are both good and bad reasons for the strikingly apolitical way in which the nation's armed force is presented and, unfortunately, thought through. These are among the good reasons:

1) In the United States, civilian authority is constitutionally distinct from, and superior to, the armed forces. The military does the bidding of the nation; that is, security is a task with which the military is charged. Even though the military customarily provides advice on security issues, politics is fundamentally done elsewhere, by civilians.[2]

2) Supporting this notion is a profound, not just American, idea that the military is a profession, perhaps even a science, and therefore somewhat more objective than, or beyond, politics.[3] Rephrased more critically, modern warfare is a preeminently bureaucratic enterprise and so aspires to a particular objectivity. This objectivity is a great strength. By the exact same token, as a bureaucratic enterprise, warfare is conducted under the banner of objective policy and so tends to eschew subjectivity and even responsibility. As we shall see, this is a great weakness, not only morally[4] but in terms of political effectiveness (bureaucracies are difficult to love or even respect).

3) More viscerally, it seems far easier to deal with the enemy—who is trying to kill us and who we are trying to kill—as not one of us, that is, as outside of our politics.[5] And, as this book will make abundantly

clear, thinking seriously about politics, especially in an age of Islamist violence and globalization, is not easy.

Despite such difficulties, I propose that we can and should consider these wars, and security policy vis-à-vis the threat of Islamist violence more generally, in the broadest political terms. For the sake of clarity, let me express myself rather abstractly, even though I am quite aware that such matters are always far more complicated. But it seems fair to begin our thinking about security from the idea that, whatever else it may be, killing represents a breach of the peace, and collectively, war represents the failure of policy to provide security, an idea as old as Sun Tzu.[6] If war represents the breakdown of the security order, then the purpose of the war, at least if it is fought by a civilized government, is to restore the peace by establishing a security order to replace the order that has collapsed.[7] As cruelly ironic, even Orwellian, as it sounds, the civilized purpose of war is to make peace.[8]

Peace lasts only so long as hostilities do not begin anew, so long as the embers of old hatreds do not flare up. Therefore, to have a lasting peace, we must find a way to live together, that is, the construction of a durable peace requires the participation of all concerned, even those who had been enemies, in the new order. This is a logical outgrowth of the idea, made justly famous after the Allied victory in World War II, that winning the war is not enough: we must win the peace.[9] But we can think further: if we regard the outbreak of war as failure, then the conduct of war is devoted to the possibility of politics, not just among the citizens of the republic but in the broader world. How we fight is always already a political act in our world, even as death ends the world for our enemies. This book attempts to show that we can use our hopes for politics, implicit in all wars, *to structure* our thinking about security, including wars we avert, and the shooting wars in which we find ourselves engaged. "The political object is the goal, war is the means of reaching it, and *means can never be considered in isolation from their purpose.*"[10]

In recent years, Joseph Nye has usefully distinguished between "hard" and "soft" power, and emphasized that American political greatness and security depended on a combination of the two. Nye has gone on to argue, rightfully, that the United States during the second Bush administration paid too little attention to soft power, and thereby weakened its strategic position. As someone occasionally engaged in public diplomacy, I could not agree more. But this book is not about soft power in contrast with, or as a complement to, hard power. Instead, I argue that even the hardest expressions of power need to be understood politically. Killing signifies to the survivors. To put the same point differently, all exercises of power—with the possible exceptions of a kept secret or a literally final solution—are also forms of speech, and therefore must be understood in terms of their reception and audience. So, and here Nye may disagree, when it comes to the exercise of power, the opinion of the audience always matters, whether the power in question is hard or soft.

ASSUMPTIONS

To be practical, a constructive account of security policy, like a business model, must address its context. Specifically, my argument rests on three admittedly troubling and broad assumptions about the situation that we, as a nation, seek to secure.

1. Islamist Violence

As already suggested, Islamist violence, whether state sponsored or not, is a real security threat. Such violence is geographically widespread; arises in both the developing world and the most contemporary of societies, including the United States; and gives every sign of being a concern for a long time. There has been immoderate talk of world war, Global Jihad, and the clash of civilizations. Such talk is unfortunate, and there is much, much more to say about Islam, but politesse should not require us to deny that many security concerns for the United States are in some sense "Islamist," just as security concerns during the Cold War were often "communist." Violent threats to the United States in our time are likely to be organized by people who speak and think in an Islamic idiom. I stress this point at the outset because it bears on one of my central arguments: the strategic significance of U.S. responses, military and otherwise, to such "Islamist" issues will be shaped by how our actions are understood by Muslims, including many Muslims who are not Americans. That is part of what it means to say that war is politics: we have to consider what our violence means, especially among our enemies and those who might be enemies.

It should be acknowledged at the outset that Islamist security issues are not the only imaginable, or necessarily the most serious, threats. It is possible, perhaps even likely, that the United States will witness the emergence of another "peer competitor," that is, a major military power organized along essentially national lines. Despite all the talk of globalization, nationalism has hardly vanished. At present, however, U.S. military capability far outstrips that of other nations, and it is hard to imagine, at least in the short to medium run, the United States fighting the kind of national conflict that defined nineteenth- and twentieth-century warfare. Or perhaps our security is more seriously threatened by environmental dangers, or a pandemic, or the unraveling of our own social fabric. Although I do not deny that there are other security concerns, surely Islamist violence, and the hot wars we are fighting, provide worry enough to merit a book.

2. Globalization

The context for Islamist violence, and for U.S. action, is essentially global, not national. By "context" I mean not only geographic extension (both Islamist violence and U.S. military power are widespread) but also political environment. Even national wars, for example Iraq, are fought within a much broader strategic field, in which only some of the actors are states—a situation neatly expressed by "al-Qaeda in Iraq." This should not be surprising: after World War II, the United States worked hard to create an integrated and, in profound respects, postnational global order that I have elsewhere called the City of Gold. This effort at globalization is now, for many purposes and for better and worse, largely achieved. The exercise of U.S. military power, then, must be analyzed and evaluated in relation to the global order that the United States has spent so much blood and treasure establishing.

U.S. security policy is global in another sense. The fulcrum on which my argument turns is that, because war is about making peace, and peace requires the participation of foreigners, the political actors are not all U.S. citizens. Since Clausewitz, we understand war as the forceful expression of the political will of the sovereign. In a democratic republic, the people are sovereign, so war is presumed to be the political will of the people, U.S. citizens.[11] We also understand war to be about the construction of a durable peace. Peace requires the political will of everyone involved, even former enemies. And in a global society, that means that political actors are everywhere. The execution of U.S. security policy, therefore, is not only what the military traditionally conceives it to be—the effort to realize national interests that are decided upon by domestic political processes. Our security policy is at the same time political action on a global stage, vis-à-vis fellow members of the global society that we, after all, have worked so hard to construct.

I therefore believe—although developing the argument would take us too far afield—that the political perspective set forth here is the best way for Americans to think about other, non-Islamist threats that may arise, not because of the nature of the threat but because such threats will arise in an essentially globalized social context. That is, the world in which the nation thinks about security requires a deeply global political perspective, regardless of the specific origin of the threats.

3. Force Projection

The United States and its allies will continue to project force globally. Such force usually will be present but not exercised. When it is exercised, the United States usually, but not always, will have the sanction of the international community, and recent history has demonstrated that the United States will use force even without such sanction. Thus, for the foreseeable future, the United States will understand its own security to be achieved best through the preservation and extension of an integrated global order, multilaterally when possible, unilaterally if necessary.

The United States is deeply committed to this global security order. Regardless of the currently widespread and understandable desire to end the wars in Afghanistan and Iraq, real limits exist on the freedom that the United States has to withdraw. This may sound strange to people, inside and outside of the United States, used to thinking of power, and maybe especially the power of the U.S. military, in terms of liberty, what it allows the U.S. government to do. However, suppose the United States withdraws in some substantial sense from Iraq. Will it maintain a presence in Kuwait? In Turkey? In the Persian Gulf? Will the United States withdraw from the Middle East altogether? What about South Asia, and in particular, what should our relationship, military and otherwise, to Pakistan be? Should the United States withdraw from the sea-lanes in the western Pacific? And so forth. Great power fosters its own constraints, and our position is soberingly akin to that of Athens prior to its loss in the Peloponnesian War. We are committed to some substantial extension, to a host of forward positions. Pericles believed Athens could secure its extended position, and he may have been right, even if history did not work out that way. This book asks analogous questions about the extension of the United States.

Although we are not free to withdraw everywhere and absolutely, it may well be that some substantial withdrawal is possible, politically required (certainly promised by the administration), and perhaps even advisable. The expansive security policy of the last decades coincided with a period of great economic prosperity. In a time of prosperity, it was decided to fight wars with government debt. As of this writing, the prosperity is gone, and the debts are becoming due. Surely fiscal constraints will hamper U.S. strategic expression?

Moreover, recent security policy has hardly been a huge success. The United States is much less popular than it once was; the nation is hated in many quarters. The wars drag on, and it is far from clear that we are getting safer. And our foreign policy has not helped as much as might like: we have bred cultures of dependence, corruption, and endemic violence where we had hoped for happy societies. For example, one could argue that, for the medium future, substantially smaller involvement in Pakistan would not only reduce our costs but encourage the social and political development that Pakistan desperately needs. Whether or not such arguments are compelling is not here the point—the point is that the argument's plausibility reminds us that engaging more deeply, in more places cannot always be in the nation's interest. Sometimes less is more.

Although conducting security policy in more restrained fashion than we have over the last decade or so might be wise, such newfound modesty should be kept in perspective. The United States is highly unlikely to withdraw to its own shores. Although the American people have a profoundly isolationist streak, the lesson of the 1920s remains: the world is simply too scary a place to be ignored. The United States will remain engaged, for its own security and for the opportunities to do good that sometimes present themselves.

Obviously, these three assumptions (Islamist violence is a substantial threat; the context for security politics is global; the U.S. will continue to project force) are contestable, and at the very least, they are quite general. Lack of space and the desire for clarity prevent me from trying to argue that these three assumptions are fundamentally sound descriptions of the world; I ask the skeptical reader to accept my description of our situation for the sake of argument. More importantly, however, this book is written for the many people, including security analysts and other policy makers, who already share these basic assumptions. That is, this book asks, if Islamist violence is a serious problem, and if the United States will secure itself by projecting military force globally, and if any such use of force must be understood as a way of doing global politics, then how should we Americans begin thinking through our use of force? How are we to construct institutions that will accomplish our aims?

TERMINOLOGY

A few words on terminology may be helpful. Various terms have been used in discussion of what this book calls Islamist violence. In general, this book uses "Islamist" to mean a political grammar, including a military grammar, that is rooted in an Islamic idiom. Under the heading "Islamist," I include various kinds of sometimes quite different politics, notably both political Islam, a form of nationalism, and radical neofundamentalism, a form of political association especially well suited to the age of globalization.[12] (Political Islam and radical neofundamentalism are discussed in more detail in Chapter Seven.) "Islamic" is used here to refer to a system of faith, roughly equivalent to "Christian." In some contrast, "Muslim" implies less about faith than about people in a place and culture—the analogous term in discussing Europe or the United States would usually but not always be "Western."[13]

And finally, what should these conflicts, collectively, be called? When discussing the perspective of the other side, I use "bin Laden's War" or sometimes "Global Jihad." When discussing our perspective on this conflict, however, there is no one good name equivalent to "Cold War." As noted, the Bush administration's "Global War on Terror" has fallen from favor, which is fortunate, since the term is too inflammatory, too general, and too chauvinistic—simply too blunt an instrument.[14] Samuel Huntington's "clash of civilizations" commits lesser sins along similar lines. The military's current phrase "overseas contingency operations" is so bureaucratic it sounds like parody.

Like counterinsurgency generally, the phrase "Long War" rightly emphasizes political will, and widespread participation, in establishing order in lieu of violent chaos. But "Long War" is also highly problematic.[15] The phrase is an old one (various wars have been long) that recently has been used to name an arc of conflict between liberal democracies and authoritarian governments over most of the twentieth century. In this grand, and rather Manichean, vision of history, liberal democracy overcame totalitarian ideologies of right and left, which, because they were totalitarian, are understood to be essentially the same. "Long War" thus echoes "Cold War," a matter of no accident in security politics.[16] But however we sort out the strengths and weaknesses of such an understanding of twentieth-century history, the analogy to our current security situation is weak. As will be explored throughout this book, our situation is not very much like the struggle against Nazi fascism, nor is it much like the Cold War. Those conflicts, for starters, were organized by states. Nor can it truly be said, as bin Laden and others have, that our conflict is with Islam or with the Muslim world. Indeed, many present security problems stem from conflicts *within* the Muslim world. And so this book uses "Islamist conflict" and cognate terms when discussing the security threats, and outright violence, informed by the global operation of political Islam and especially radical neofundamentalism.

CHAPTER TWO

LOOKING INWARD

National Interests vs.
Bureaucratic Objectives

PRAGMATIC INTENTIONS

In thinking about security, even combat operations, in political terms, I want to be as practical and constructive as I possibly can. This book is intended neither as an abstract theoretical exercise nor as an analysis of recent U.S. actions. This book does not demonstrate my professional skills as an academic or as a lawyer: I have written not only clearly but unguardedly, and while there is a reasonably extensive bibliography, the notes have been kept to a bare minimum, by way of convenience. If I think something is important, I have tried to say it in the text, plainly.

In this book, I hope to develop a critical perspective, a judgmental stance, that can be used by both experts and voters to defend some ways of conducting security policy and, conversely, that can provide a coherent basis for criticizing other ways of doing things. We Americans should be able to explain to ourselves and to others why these ways of securing ourselves are worthy of the deepest imaginable support—lives. Such thinking, and such communication, takes place within a conceptual frame; this book is an effort to articulate the frame.

THINKING THROUGH SECURITY POLICY

As with any policy, security policy should be evaluated on its substance. Is this activity, this exercise of power, what we, as a democratic republic, wish to be done in our name, and at the cost of other goals? Simply put, is this security policy a worthy use of the nation's power? This question may seem straightforward, but in the life of the republic, the question of the appropriateness of this or that security policy has proven to be conceptually difficult. Here are three interrelated reasons for our difficulties in discussing what would seem, perhaps, the most basic of political questions:

First, in the broad sense, "security" is not a controversial policy at all. Few Americans would argue with the proposition that defending the nation is an important, perhaps the most important, obligation of government.

Second, security policy contains the possibility of war, and with it, the loss of life. This, too, is a reality that the United States has borne throughout its history. And now as then, most Americans are willing to say that security demands things that are not, at bottom, respectable or worthy, that are in fact almost unbearably sad—young soldiers sent to die and, worse, to commit horrors, maybe euphemistically called "collateral damage," and nobody's desired policy. Thus the security context routinely presents arguments from necessity: "we acknowledge that what have done is deeply unfortunate, but it was required by national security," and so on.

Third, such arguments are sometimes true but are almost invariably *convenient* for the military and civilian bureaucrats charged with making and implementing security policy and to the vast economic interests who sell to such bureaucrats, what Eisenhower famously called the military-industrial complex.[1] There are bad people; buy this weapon. In some circumstances this advice is wise, but not in all situations, and who is to say? Experts, of course—the question of what is actually militarily necessary is often asserted to be professional rather than political, a matter for the executive and therefore decided by the security community rather than by more democratic, transparent, and less self-interested institutions. There are opportunities for corruption here, of course, but the world is too primitive, too moral, for a sclerosis of willful ignorance and interested self-deception. Despite an ethos of national service that is widespread in the security community and very real, the extent to which members of that community are capable of making good decisions about whether the policy of the republic is respectable is and always should remain open to question, especially because we have a professionalized security apparatus. This is why Eisenhower warned us: in a bureaucratized military, served by large corporations (also bureaucracies, governed through offices), the danger is unlikely to be men and women of bad faith. Instead, the danger we face is that our servants—those who serve—do not understand our business, confuse their institutional objectives with the national interest, and, being experts, do not feel obliged to listen.

Thus, while it may at first sound quite banal for me to propose that, in a democratic republic, security policy should be questioned just as other policies are questioned, in our actual political practice, security policy is unselfconsciously understood to be (1) desirable (in terms of its general objective, the security of Americans) and (2) sadly necessary (in terms of this or that specific action), at least as "necessary" is determined by those experts entrusted with (and often professionally and or financially benefited by) such decisions, and therefore (3) beyond question by nonexperts, that is, voters or even other experts, and hence beyond politics. The logical structure of security arguments easily can be used to prove too much and to justify any military action, any exercise of domestic authority, and, profoundly if prosaically importantly, any expenditure, as we have seen in recent years.

To say that security policy tends to be viewed as desirable, necessary, and rather beyond question is not to say that wars are not opposed in the United States; they are. This nation has a long tradition of Quakers and other pacifists who are against war on principle. More particularly, after the Vietnam War, many people were deeply suspicious of the presidency and of the security community. This rift never entirely healed, and old wounds in the body politic have been reopened by the wars in Iraq and Afghanistan, which have lost popularity with age. Since 9/11 and the passage of the Patriot Act and other laws, of course, security has been a pervasive justification for governmental action. Security concerns have informed controversies over airports, assassinations, border crossings into friendly countries like Canada and Mexico, libraries, rendition, surveillance, the suspension of *habeas corpus*, torture, and so on. Many of these initiatives are, to put it mildly, more or less controversial.

But most such opposition to security measures takes place on grounds that are somewhat *outside* the logic of security policy. For example, we may simply oppose war because God said, "Thou shalt not kill," as the King James version has it.[2] Or, for another example, we often engage in balancing, in which we say that some (usually impossible to specify) gain in security is or is not worth some (difficult to specify) loss of civil liberty. While these positions may be sound, such objections to security policy are external; that is, they do not rest on a judgment of security policy as such and on its own terms.

Such objections tend to be absolute, leading to decisions of yes or no. If we are to have a security policy, or more bluntly, if we are going to exercise force, and have thus decided to participate in violence to some (what?) extent, such external standards are of little help in assessing the substance of our policy. The question remains: is our security policy respectable, *is this use of violence worthy of us*? Is this how we as a republic should deploy ourselves? To answer that, we need to think *through* what we mean by a given security policy, not simply vote yes or no. We need standards of judgment *internal* to the logic of security, yet expressive of the national—as opposed to the narrow, bureaucratic—interest.

For example, from the perspective of a bureaucracy charged with the elimination of particular known terrorists, or individuals that a foreign intelligence service asserts are terrorists, running a program of assassination by drone in countries in which we are not officially at war might make sense. Whether such assassinations actually contribute to the security of the United States is hardly a question, because by hypothesis, the elimination of those who would harm the United States helps the United States. Even less-often asked is whether such presumed contributions to the security of the nation are worth the cost, economically, politically, and, sometimes, in blood, of maintaining the shape and size of our footprint in South Asia. Even less-often asked is whether we wish to be a nation that targets others, and sometimes its own citizens, on the basis of what is, no doubt, the best available intelligence, surely better than rumor albeit without the formalities of judicial process, in places where we are not at war. In short, from the perspective of certain bureaucracies, to become a nation of bumbling assassins makes perfect sense. Nearly ten years on, bin Laden remains at large, even though we've taken out some buses and wedding parties and no doubt quite a few actual terrorists. But war has always been very messy, and as over a half century of history has rather conclusively demonstrated, the intelligence bureaucracies can neither be seriously be relied on to be very good at what is, after all, an extraordinarily difficult task, nor be expected to acknowledge their own weaknesses unless compelled by yet another debacle, for which excuses will be made. Most importantly of all, such bureaucracies are, by definition, composed of putative experts, who are not charged with understanding what it means to be the republic.

The widely felt need for an intellectual standard with which bureaucratic security policy may be judged does much to explain the recent revival of interest, across the political spectrum, in the churchman and public intellectual Reinhold Niebuhr, who served as a tough-minded voice of conscience in the Depression and through much of the Cold War.[3] Niebuhr recognized that in the struggle against Nazi and then Soviet totalitarianism, the United States would employ military force. Indeed, Niebuhr believed that the United States was right to meet force with force, and he strenuously opposed contemporary liberals who failed to recognize and contest the evils then abroad in the world. At the same time, Niebuhr also understood that power, even when legitimately exercised, always presents temptations and that, therefore, the exercise of military force always requires critical vigilance. So, for liberals who recognize that force is necessary in today's world but also recognize that the exercise of force must be held to some honorable standard, Niebuhr is an attractive figure.

Niebuhr's vigilance was impelled by his awareness, first, of the limited nature of humanity, broadly speaking, by the inescapability of sin. Second, for Niebuhr human limitation was not only a matter of individual morality. Nations were even less perfectible than individuals, and the unwinnable struggle of politics was to make the nation's collective actions virtuous. Third, Niebuhr understood history to be providential, the unfolding of God's plan, which could be discerned, if often only dimly. From the perspective of providential history, U.S. policy could be judged—had the nation played its role on the earth well? Power, then, even the awesome power of the United States in possession of nuclear weapons, was not an ultimate standard. In his recognition of evil, his willingness to use force in compromised circumstances, his understanding of the temptations and other limitations of power, and especially his effort to provide a context through which the exercise of military power could be judged, Niebuhr's teachings are indeed relevant to our situation.

At the same time, however, Niebuhr's politics drew on cultural resources, particularly shared understandings, that are now less available to the United States. Despite the joking yet deeply complimentary phrase "atheists for

Niebuhr," he spoke and wrote for a nation whose political classes were over-whelmingly if not always rigorously Protestant and who were, therefore, in a position to hear the lessons that Niebuhr tried to deliver. While Protestant thinking remains an essential aspect of U.S. politics, this cannot fairly be called a WASP nation, and national political discourse cannot base itself on assumptions of shared Protestant understandings of sin or of the place of man in history. More importantly still, the politics in question is not solely American. In projecting force globally, the United States seeks to do politics in foreign, and often Muslim, contexts. Crafting a self-consciously political security policy under the various conditions the world presents will require more than a return to Niebuhr, as useful as (re)reading Niebuhr is.

As discussed in the preceding chapter, this book argues that common understandings of politics, understood in broadly participatory terms but on a global scale, can inform, organize, and discipline our thinking about the use of force. What would it mean for our tactics, strategy, and institutions to conceptualize security policy in terms of politics understood to be a human activity found *everywhere*? I argue, and hope this book demonstrates, that a rather everyday understanding of politics can provide a normative horizon for our thinking about military force. Rephrased, "politics" can do for contemporary U.S. thinking about the nation's violence what "providential history" did—or might have done—for the tough-minded liberalism of the Cold War era, that is, lay the foundations for a position from which to justify our decisions to leash or let slip the dogs of war.

Specifically, we can and should demand the following of our public servants in their conduct of security policy on our behalf:

Be effective. It is difficult, perhaps impossible, to justify security policy that is ineffective, that is not rationally related to the ends the nation is trying to achieve. It must immediately be added that security policy, including military policy, is not all of war, and certainly not all of violence. The rage of Achilles or Chief Joseph's desperate retreat bear remembering.[4] Such examples of violence contain their own profound, indeed existential, logic. But by the same token, such violence is not military policy, not professional or bureaucratic, and not, in that sense, rational. For present purposes, it is enough to insist that this nation, which aspires to be an enlightened democratic republic with professional diplomatic and military bureaucracies, should call its security policy to account for its effectiveness, as it does with other policies. Are the ways in which we conduct ourselves tactically, operationally, and strategically likely to be effective?

But effective at what? It would seem clear that we want our security institutions to be effective at achieving the *national* interests at stake. In practice, however, this objective is not clear at all. As suggested above, bureaucracies are logically structured around narrow institutional missions. To this, one might add that warriors are existentially dependent on their enemies. So, for both warriors and bureaucrats, killing the enemy all too easily becomes a murderous end in itself, without justification. To kill people or help others kill people, even bad people like, for instance, the Soviets who invaded Afghanistan or people we are told are terrorists or at least associate with terrorists, for the sake of killing enemies, while perhaps piously hoping that good politics might simply follow, is fundamentally irresponsible. (It is also a sin, a transgression for which we are being punished.)

Let me be clear at the risk of a certain redundancy: bureaucracy poses durable problems for republican security policy. Bureaucracies have missions, and correctly tend to define their own effectiveness in terms of their success at accomplishing their specific mission, for topical example, to take control of a city, achieve air supremacy, or simply to do harm to the nation's enemies or at least its military and intelligence services. From a national perspective, however, such missions are means, not ends. Controlling a city or the air or killing a spy on the other side may be required to impose a security order. It is not, however, the security order itself. Indeed, the interests of the bureaucracy and the nation may be at odds, because fulfilling an agency's mission, for example, assassinating a terrorist, may have broad political costs. Generally speaking, the nation, not the agency, bears such costs.

If, on balance, national, as distinct from bureaucratic, interests are not served, then we cannot truthfully speak of the agency's effectiveness. Aimless acts are, in principle, ineffective, because effectiveness can only be discussed in terms of aims, which are nationally defined.

Be respectable. Effectiveness and respectability have a tight relationship in the context of security policy, precisely because security is a political endeavor. In particular, and as will be discussed in great detail throughout this book, a security policy that is not respectable cannot be persuasive in the Islamic world and therefore is ultimately ineffective, that is, cannot secure our strategic objectives. (The young man or woman who would become a terrorist is already watching.) Rephrased, it is not merely that our wars express our politics; our violence also should be understood in terms of its significance among our enemies and others that we would impress. Making operations respectable so that they are politically persuasive and therefore effective requires Americans to understand that national actions are politically significant far beyond the borders of the United States and that sensible U.S. policy will have to plan and conduct itself accordingly.

Be responsive. Not all wars are the same. War, too, has a history and even an anthropology. In the present context, under the broad heading of "Islamist violence," the United States finds itself embroiled in tribal conflicts, nationalist struggles, and terrorist operations that presume globalization. These conflicts may share Islamist rhetoric, and there is considerable overlap between these and other kinds of warfare (the hearts of warriors need not be ideologically pure), but it is important to realize that our wars differ in kind, because they are waged by different sorts of polity. Our stance vis-à-vis our enemies, and indeed vis-à-vis others in the world, must be informed by our understanding of their various political situations. U.S. wars in Vietnam and Iraq are very different, but both were marked by horribly belated understandings of local politics, and therefore the nature of the war in which we were engaged. To put matters gently, strategy, operations, and even tactics suffered as a result and lives were wasted.

Insofar as war can be justified at all, it is justified by its end. What sort of order are we fighting to bring about? Can we achieve that end; that is, can the war be won? This question is fundamentally political, although an affirmative answer means that military conditions must be met. The essentially political nature of the problem should be obvious, but it evidently is not. As this book goes to press, after years and years of fighting in Afghanistan and Iraq, a welcome consensus has at last emerged that we are fighting an insurgency and that success must be secured "politically" rather than "conventionally." But we are a long way from understanding what that means in theater, to say nothing of in the broader world. As the Iraq war dragged on, defenders of the U.S. effort, including commanding general Tommy Franks, found themselves arguing that we won the war ("mission accomplished," etc.), but we just were not ready for the "follow-on" peace.[5] This is equivalent to a company dividing its manufacturing processes from the "follow-on" product, or a nation dividing its elections from the "follow-on" government. The peace we actually achieve is the purpose of our war, the only justification for what is otherwise merely killing.

Create good institutions. Doing good work requires the right tools. Serious thought about what we, as a people, wish to achieve when we enter wastelands of our own creation cannot help but call our institutions into question. If we wish to achieve great things in education, we must ask after our schools. If we wish to decide our conflicts fairly, we cannot ignore the health of the courts and the training of lawyers. If we wish to conduct foreign policy, including the projection of force, appropriately, we must ask whether our institutions are capable of accomplishing our objectives.

Such questions are not to be resolved by this or any other book. This book articulates considerations to be confronted, difficulties to be managed, temptations to be acknowledged—aspects of our situation that we ignore at our peril. But while politics will remain devilishly difficult, the standards themselves are fairly clear. A security policy worthy of the name, by which I mean an exercise in collective political thought rather than an excuse for the exercise of force in fact, must be

- effective;
- respectable;
- responsive to its war, including the enemy, and all others concerned;
- able to construct a peace; and
- conducted by appropriate institutions.

How well our current institutions measure up to these standards I leave to the reader's judgment.

CHAPTER THREE

OVERVIEW OF
THE ARGUMENT

This book makes the following argument.

To understand foreign policy (to include security policy, and even more dramatically, the waging of war) in political terms requires us to think about the exercise of U.S. power as unavoidably political dealings with foreigners and sometimes enemies, people who are also fellow inhabitants of global society. *In global society, U.S. security policy is global politics.*

But common habits of mind incline us to think about security in cramped fashion, that is, nationally rather than globally, or not to think politically at all. Our capacity to act on the oft-quoted idea that war is a form of political expression has been hampered by widespread but unacknowledged assumptions about the nature of politics at issue in our confrontation with Islamist violence, "prejudices" in the literal sense of the word. Each of these assumptions tends to obscure the political work that our security situation, in fact, requires us to do. As a result of being obscured, the politics of security is hardly thought through in any serious sense. Indeed, in the conduct of security policy since 9/11, politics often seemed quite beside the point—this is a war, it was said.

Recently, it has become common to acknowledge that we need to succeed politically as well as militarily in Afghanistan and Iraq, and implicitly in Pakistan and other Muslim lands and in non-Muslim countries like the

United States. Notably, in Afghanistan and Iraq, we have taken steps to reduce civilian casualties, and more generally, we have attempted to make our interventions more sensitive to their human context, and therefore, we hope, more effective. While this change of stance represents real progress, a vast distance separates abstract recognition of the need for a political solution, or even the cultural sensitivity entailed in classical counterinsurgency doctrine, and the practical doing of politics, not only in Afghanistan and Iraq but across the Muslim world. We may have finally wandered onto the plain, but we have as yet no more than begun to cross it.

Lip service will not suffice. Politics is never beside the point in war, and certainly not in the security policy that encompasses and makes possible combat operations. Politics is the point. We miss this all too easily, and because we do not understand security as essentially political, much needful political work has not been done. Time and again, the United States has missed opportunities for political engagement, and hence failed to achieve its security objectives. This is not entirely new. Our victories notwithstanding, we have had notable losses since World War II, both on the battlefield and in the fabric of our politics, and many "victories" have been pyrrhic or simply not worth it. Again, this book does not undertake a critical review of security policy since, say, 1945, but simply proceeds from the assumption that our security policy has been far less effective than we reasonably might have hoped, an assumption that might be labeled "Vietnam," "9/11," or "torture." If we are to have a security policy that confronts Islamist violence as a political issue across a global context, we might start by rethinking the patterns of thought that prevent us from thinking politically. Part Two, "Aspects of Engagement," begins that task.

What do I mean by "prejudices" or "obstacles to thought"? To oversimplify for the sake of clarity, we Americans tend to understand Islamist violence in terms of familiar political imaginations, notably of the state or of crime (Chapter Four, "Naming the Enemy"). Or we understand instability in the Islamic world as a symptom of some other, more fundamental, issue that we can in principle identify, thereby resolving our conflicts with Islamist adversaries (Chapter Five, "Political Subjects"). We often understand ourselves to be farther down history's road than the Islamic world is, implying that the problem will go away if we simply wait, and that therefore no serious political engagement is necessary or even possible (Chapter Six, "Politics Is Now"). Conversely, we fail to understand Islamists, even radicals, as our contemporaries, who are also trying to be modern (Chapter Seven, "The Modernism of Radical Neofundamentalism"). And we understand security in terms of its opposite, violence, and violence in terms of bad people—"the terrorists," who should, of course, be addressed kinetically, that is, killed. We implicitly assume that an orderly politics will somehow arise in their absence (Chapter Eight, "All Politics Is Spatial").

In a perfectly logical world, each of these prejudices would preclude political engagement. To engage politically, we must look beyond ourselves; we must recognize our fellows ("citizens"); we must understand our citizens to operate in the present; we must recognize that we are all trying to construct a future, the "what is to be done?" of politics; and we must share a conception of space—this city; this republic; this globe, which is governed in certain ways; the law of this place. In our own less than logically rigorous world, our prejudices make political engagement—and so security policy properly understood—simply much more difficult than it need be. This book attempts to demonstrate that these prejudices are wrong, at least wrong *for the doing of politics*, and should be reined in, thereby opening the door to richer engagement with the world in which we would be secure.

Part Three, "The Challenge of Radical Neofundamentalism," asks what rethinking Islamist violence in particular, and security policy generally, means in political terms for U.S. policy. Global Jihad, the violence of radical neofundamentalism, is different—in its relationship to ordinary politics, in its signification, and, consequently, in its strategic consequences—from the violence of state actors (Chapter Nine, "Bin Laden's Challenge"). Critically, the reformulation of Islamist violence in political, that is, ideological, terms means that the key actor is not the terrorist but the audience. While violence is inescapably conceived of bilaterally (on the image of the duel), bin Laden's War is more significantly performative and thus has a triangular structure: offense, defense, and audience.

Substantively, therefore, at the strategic level, we are engaged in a conflict over narratives of modernity (Chapter Ten, "Ideological Abstraction and Concrete Presence"). At this level of abstraction, our situation is not entirely new: foreign policy may quite traditionally and normatively be understood as an effort to promulgate our idea of what "being modern" means. Practically, foreign policy may be conducted through diplomacy, trade, and other peaceful endeavors (Chapter Eleven, "Peacetime Contests") or through violence (Chapter Twelve, "Wartime Contests").

Part Four, "Institutional Reform," argues that the institutional structure of our security community is not well suited for foreign policy as this book conceives the enterprise. Chapter Thirteen, "New World Security," assumes what we are constantly told, that this is a new world, very different from the Cold War world, and further assumes that much of this book's argument about politics and security has been somewhat persuasive. If these two assumptions hold, it would be truly astonishing if the bureaucratic structure established to fight the Cold War was well suited to accomplish contemporary national objectives. In fact, the Cold War apparatus is fundamentally outmoded and should be redesigned.

In the global context, a range of nonstate actors play vital roles, and much of our political intercourse is not polite. If the United States is to have a coordinated foreign policy, it needs a bureaucracy with power and scope. The Department of State should be reconstituted, with more money and broader responsibility, and renamed the Department of Foreign Affairs (Chapter Fourteen).

By the same token, in a world without a peer competitor, the Department of Defense is not about defense. In a world in which the United States engages in preemptive wars, military operations are not justified as self-defense.[1] Within constitutional bounds, the military should reconceive its job to be political in the sense of establishing and maintaining order and of fostering a safe global society. To that end, the Department of Defense should be renamed the Department of Military Operations (Chapter Fifteen).

The idea of intelligence as an independent function of government, not moored to diplomatic or military concerns, is antithetical to a responsible polity. Although secrets cannot be banished from human affairs, a government that operates extensively through secrecy and establishes agencies on that basis is not seriously asking for the participation of others. Secrets are literally irresponsible; they preclude the assumption of responsibility. Therefore, intelligence should be done by accountable agencies of the U.S. government, as it has been throughout the nation's history with the exception of the Cold War and the roughly two decades since the Cold War ended. In particular, the CIA should be abolished, and its worthy functions assigned to the Departments of Foreign Affairs and Military Operations (Chapter Sixteen, "The Reintegration of Intelligence").

Finally, in a brief conclusion, I speculate on our prospects.

TOPICS AVOIDED

I have limited this book in a number of ways that initially may seem odd, but the reasons for my choices should become clear enough. In particular, I have avoided the following.

Partisan Politics

I do not wish to spend any more time than clarity requires criticizing our conduct of the wars in Afghanistan and Iraq. The reason for this is simple: all too easily, discussion of U.S. security policy descends into partisan bickering. Without mincing words, our national discourse on these wars has been appalling, not only because of what has been said but in our widespread inability to listen to others, an inability that also has other sources and that has now spawned its own clichés: the red state/blue state, the cultural divide, and so forth. Perhaps it was ever thus—this nation plunged into its Civil War based on name-calling and idiotic suppositions. But I also think that some contemporary partisanship is new, that political discourse has been transformed within my adult lifetime.[2] Candidates are routinely treated like players for their teams, sometimes "Democrats" or "Republicans," but more often "conservatives" or "progressives" and the like. The language of policy argument is widely used for what amounts to cheerleading. And just as very intelligent people may devote themselves to football or other sports, very intelligent people can spend endless time and energy on "politics," that is, on the progress or setbacks of their team and on crafting "arguments" designed to benefit their side. But thinking to a predetermined end is not thinking at all: it may be preaching to the choir or advocacy, but it hardly helps us explore what we do not know, for example, the question of what is to be done. And when, as now, the question of what is to be done is truly difficult, we are the poorer.

To make matters worse, the practice of politics as a somewhat intellectual and very competitive sport undermines actual political discourse, understood as the collective activity at the heart of the democratic dream. When we know what side people are on, we know roughly what they will say and whether we will oppose or support it, and thus we have no need to listen to them. Who listens to the cheerleaders for the other side? Democracy has always been a rough-and-tumble enterprise, and I do not wish to be naive. But television and the "responsible press" simply did not always have the sort of nakedly name-calling, baiting excuses for argument about vital matters (remember, the question on the table is whether we, as a nation, should go kill people) that now pass for discussion of the issues. And we as Americans know, or at least once knew, that. In 1977, in a *Saturday Night Live* parody of a regular segment on a news show, Dan Ackroyd said to Jane Curtin, "Jane, you ignorant slut." It was, as satire should be, funny and edgy.[3] We knew we were approaching a line, since crossed, not only in what was acceptable on television but in how we understood the relationship between entertainment and politics.

My purpose here is republican in the ancient sense: I want to say some things of use to the body politic. Obviously, my purpose is also democratic: I am trying to offer up years of my thought for whatever use such thoughts may be to the electorate of which I am a member. This is why I eschew the "objective" stance of the critic and instead use "we" throughout this text. I mean we in the United States, we Americans, who vote and who are ultimately answerable for the killing done in our name. I admit to being a bit nostalgic, certainly idealistic. But I do believe that Americans are wiser and more humane than our political discourse now indicates. We can have a better politics. And that is all I have to say about partisanship.

Law

A venerable discourse, the law of war (*jus ad bellum*), concerns whether or not wars may be justified or condemned, as the case may be. An almost equally venerable discourse, the law in war (*jus in bello*), concerns what may, or may not, be done in war. Despite their applicability to the deployment of U.S. force, the laws in and of war are only tangentially related to the question at issue in this book. Even when true, the claims (and foreign ministries, including our State Department, are duty-bound to claim) that a given war is legal and is being prosecuted in legally acceptable ways, tell us little about the wisdom of the foreign policy expressed through the war. Law sets bounds to what is permissible but says much less about what is advisable. Very many dreadful mistakes are perfectly legal; consider failed mergers, marriages, or monetary policies. So, even heroically assuming that the

United States henceforth obtains Security Council approval for its wars, the question of how to run security policy would remain. And if we ask not whether this war is legal but the broader and deeper questions of how security policy is to be conducted, that is, what stance we should take toward our fears and what institutions are required to realize such intentions, then the laws in and of war have almost nothing to say.

The foregoing paragraph is exaggerated for clarity. The law has a great deal to teach but only for those with ears to hear and a certain consciousness of their own formation. History, extending back through the Cold War, has by now persuasively demonstrated that, for those who make security policy, law—here meaning the law of war embodied in and derived from the UN Charter and associated documents—does not govern security questions. For those charged with security, law is not the answer. Law is at best an afterthought.[4] This book therefore does not argue *from* the law.[5]

In a different way, however, this book will argue *toward* the law. The global order we have worked so hard to establish is a highly legalistic order. I do not believe "the rule of law" is an unmitigated good, but it is a central commitment of the sorts of modernity that the United States has struggled to achieve. Our foreign policy, including our military policy, should therefore act to strengthen the legal order, including the laws in and of war.

Particular Judgments

Contemporary political life is marked by the fact that many people (pundits, journalists generally, and even law professors, for example) have an annoying tendency to argue with great certitude about distant matters for which they are not responsible. I suspect this is therapeutic. We like to believe we are taking a prominent stand in a world in which we are not particularly important, and more deeply, we try to convince ourselves that we are not alone, that others think and feel like we do. Much of what passes for political thought is not merely a rearrangement of prejudices, it is a search for friends, as a tour of the blogosphere dishearteningly demonstrates.

Insofar as we care about policy, however, such gratuitous exercises of particular judgment are almost always mistakes. Judgments happen in contexts. I am not an official and certainly not a military commander. Nor do I have intimate knowledge of the constraints and opportunities presented by this or that specific situation. Indeed, as suggested by the epigraph to this book, I am thankful that many hard decisions are not mine to make. So, for example, this book contains no direct advice on the extent to which disengagement from, or intensified engagement in, Afghanistan or Iraq is desirable, and if we should disengage, how and when to do so. There are any number of people, some of them in positions of power, who know (or certainly should know) more about our situation in and capabilities regarding such countries than I do and who are in a better position to make practical decisions.

The fact that we intellectuals should avoid being unduly certain about distant decisions made by others does not mean, however, that we should not make judgments, as intellectuals and especially as citizens. In a democracy, it is given to the people to judge the performance of their government. And this entire book is about how to assess our capability for violence, and the political structures that might help us to carry out foreign policy, even violent foreign policy, in as worthy a fashion as possible. It is true that to discuss the law is not to decide a case, that to study military science is not to command a company, and that economic policy does not determine business decisions. But these limitations do not mean that jurisprudence, a professional military, and a sensible economic policy are unnecessary. The context of judgment, the thinking that we do long before we must make practical decisions, the standards by which we condemn or praise particular exercises of governmental power—such is the terrain of democratic discourse and of the intellectual who attempts democratic service.[6]

PART TWO

ASPECTS OF ENGAGEMENT

CHAPTER FOUR

NAMING THE ENEMY

Security policy turns on an imagination of the enemy. Enemies must be identified and understood at least deeply enough to be recognized in order to be fought and, more to the point, in order that we may plan for the eventuality of war and lesser disturbances. How do we imagine the enemy that our planning seeks to neutralize? The activity of warfare is thus structured by the division between enemy and friend, by the division between those people whom we seek to thwart, if necessary by killing, and those we seek to protect or at least not harm. Thus, even in its conception, warfare is profoundly symmetric, a symmetry neatly expressed by the old image of war as a duel.

However, as has been widely remarked, Islamist conflicts are asymmetric, which means at least that these wars are fought among parties organized in different ways. To say that a war is structurally asymmetric suggests a basic problem for thinking about security: the situation must be recast, the ensemble bifurcated into enemies and others, in order to achieve the symmetry required for the conduct of war. The problem is familiar in the tactical and operational context of counterinsurgency: who among the people is Viet Cong, al-Qaeda in Iraq, or Taliban? Who may be targeted? But the problem is also strategic: who is the enemy against whom security policy writ large is arrayed?

To make matters much more difficult, and as will become much clearer through this book, the problem is by definition fluid. The Viet Cong, al-Qaeda, or the Taliban are loose organizations and their membership, effectiveness, and durability are not stable, much less constant. The point of counterinsurgency is to impede or discourage affiliation with such organizations and thereby to keep the insurgency from growing and eventually to make our enemy so irrelevant that they effectively disappear. And if we frame security not by organization but in the traditional geographic way, as ordered in places like Vietnam, Iraq, or Afghanistan, then the questions of who the enemy is, who may become or cease being enemies, or what contributes to an orderly peace become very fluid indeed. And if we enlarge the scope of the inquiry yet again and ask globally and vis-à-vis that constellation of violence that I am calling Islamist violence (what are the fears from which policy seeks to secure us?), then the question is subtle, multifaceted, and continual—constantly to be reasked.

The problem is terrible because it is much more than urgently practical; it is also existential. As Clausewitz taught, immediate tactical imperatives and the complexities of political life may obscure long-term strategic objectives.[1] Our immediate need to identify "the terrorists" so that we may take action, coupled with the unstable composition of "the enemy," means that we must constantly reimagine, and so redefine, our enemies. The moral, political, and hence strategic risks of constantly redefining one's enemies, and so who is killed, and so the war, and so the peace, are obvious: our immediate need to respond often leads to irrevocable actions. Bureaucratically, these problems are confronted through constant reworking, and argument over the implementation, of the rules of engagement. Yet the fact that we are rushed by circumstances into action that we may later regret hardly makes the problem—how do we imagine, describe, and so define our enemies?—disappear. Although perhaps lethally resolved for some actors, in deciding who may be targeted, we make commitments about the peace we are constructing and who we are willing to hurt to do so and thus how our exercise of force will be judged. In naming the enemy, prosecuting the war, and constructing the peace with its attendant political order, we are also constituting ourselves. We are assuming grave responsibility.

Perhaps unsurprisingly, we tend to resist this labor and take shelter in familiar conceptions. By treating states who harbor terrorists as enemy states, the "Bush doctrine" (as announced against Afghanistan but also employed with regard to Iraq and, diplomatically, Libya and Syria) attempted to give the United States and other modern militaries, organized by and around territorial states with bureaucratic command structures, a homologous opponent—another state. Yet despite the Bush doctrine, the present conflict cannot be encompassed by the traditional grammar of international relations among states. The presence of al-Qaeda operatives in Germany, Great Britain, and, of course, here in the United States has not led to war in those places, and whatever worries about the reduction of civil liberties are warranted, martial law has not been declared. The nature of the present conflict in such places requires an imagination centered on something besides the state.

But the habit of understanding war as an activity of the state—and therefore, explaining violence in terms of a *raison d'etat*—dies hard. The law of war over the last few hundred years has been conceived in terms of cross-border conflicts. For a relatively recent example, the International Court of Justice in its *Israeli Wall* advisory opinion, over some objection by Judge Rosalyn Higgins, analyzed UN Charter Article 51's right to self-defense, and hence the justifiable use of force, in terms of armed attacks by one state against another.[2] Similarly, from a perhaps ethnocentric understanding of war, it has been maintained that al-Qaeda is not a state, and therefore, al-Qaeda's violence does not constitute a war. Instead of war, we are confronted with large-scale violent crime. This, indeed, was more or less the U.S. government's position up until 9/11. Versions of this argument are still presented by human rights advocates, who seek to use the rights afforded criminal defendants to limit the powers of governments, especially that of the U.S. government.

Without denying that terrorist acts are crimes, or that the methods of law enforcement are invaluable in waging the present conflict, or that the powers of governments should be limited, it seems perversely formalistic to claim that only collective violence organized among states deserves the appellation "war." There are many ways of organizing people to fight collectively; not all such forms of organization are states. This is an age not only of terrorism but of ethnic violence, even genocide, and of slaughter in places where states have failed. Are such affairs not wars? For his part, bin Laden has always called this conflict a war. And after 9/11, the sheer violence of the attacks; the scale of the sometimes classical military responses (invasion, regime change); and the understanding that terrorism, perhaps coupled with weapons of mass destruction (WMD) technology, is a central security concern make it impossible to consider this conflict exclusively in terms familiar from criminal law enforcement. Bin Laden has a war, and he has the bodies to prove it.[3]

Even Westerners who understand this conflict as a war, albeit one not between states, often implicitly imagine warfare as an activity of a state-like entity, presumed to be rational in familiar ways. When they seek to rationalize violence by speaking of the purposes of the terrorists, in effect searching for a *raison d'etat*, Westerners generally presume that this conflict is undertaken according to familiar political logics. And *post hoc* rationalizations for terrorist violence can always be found; indeed rationalizations are often suggested by terrorists themselves. So it is variously said that terrorist violence is motivated by the victim's support for Israel, or the invasion of Afghanistan or Iraq, or the stationing of troops in Saudi Arabia, or the worldwide conspiracy against Islam in general. Terrorists can thus be understood to be carrying forth a political program through violent means (all terrorists read Clausewitz).

For those, non-Muslims and Muslims alike, trying to understand Global Jihad, this view of the situation can be deeply comforting, not just a lack of imagination. From this perspective, the logic of war is that of ordinary politics, if perhaps pursued through extraordinary means. Therefore, if we wipe away the blood, violence can be understood as if it were just another political argument. Terrorists have their grievances; that is why they become terrorists. Such arguments can easily be abstracted and rendered anodyne. Al-Qaeda's violence is often discussed in terms familiar from Western political discourse: anti-imperialism, national self-determination, the resentment bred by poverty, and so forth. The various consequences of violent acts are thus domesticated, even obscured entirely, by the translation of violence into familiar political language.

The comfort such translations might bring, however, is not without costs for the imagination and so conduct of policy. If violence is just primitive political argument, then achievement of their political objectives would make violence unnecessary for terrorists. Understanding terrorism in terms of the state (ordinary political science) presents stark alternative outcomes. The war may be ended by some form of accommodation, that is, the terrorists may win their arguments, or perhaps conversion (Americans should recall the battle for the "hearts and minds" of the Vietnamese people), that is, the terrorists may decide that they were wrong and agree with us. Or the war may be ended by identifying and incapacitating those who make such arguments, that is, the terrorists may be destroyed. But if al-Qaeda is *not* like a state, if its violence is *not* like an argument, and if its adherents are not like the soldiers of a national army, much less a debate team, then this mode of policy analysis is deeply wrongheaded, ethnocentric in the worst way.

Ethnocentricity is difficult to avoid, and it may be merely human to translate the shocking into familiar terms. For example, after the attacks of July 7, 2005, Londoners recalled World War II, in which "freedom" was pitted against "tyranny." In response, Londoners again bravely vowed not to be intimidated.[4] But were matters so simple as an opposition between the pleasures of freedom and the horrors of tyranny, an organized enemy would not even exist. Confronted with violence, we utter banal generalities and then repeat ourselves. We often insist that the strange is, in fact, familiar and that we already understand what is actually shocking, like the fact that those huge twin towers are simply not there any more. So the Bush doctrine insisted that states are responsible for war, as they have been traditionally; so terrorists are presumed to understand their violence in terms familiar from Clausewitz, as politics by other means; and so al-Qaeda is compared to the Nazis. While one must sympathize, one must also realize that such longing for the comfort of familiar thinking and rhetoric is likely to obscure what is important about the new and strange.

The tacit refusal to confront the new is nowhere more clear than in the Bush administration's "Global War on Terror," which recalled wars on other abstractions, such as drugs, poverty, and crime. Like those other wars, the war on terror, from the outset, seemed somewhat unwinnable, sort of a war on unhappiness to be specified by the commitments of the speaker. Predictably enough, rather old arguments about the nature of happiness and the purposes of government were updated for the current situation. For example, liberals maintained that we should get after the root causes of terrorism, in short, poverty. But nobody really believes that poverty per se caused the conspiracy to knock down the Twin Towers. After all, the enterprise cost too much money. Conversely, too many poor people are not violent. At least so far, the desperately poor and deeply Muslim country of Bangladesh has produced few if any international terrorists. From within the discourse of partisan politics in the United States, however, such objections matter little: "poverty" is simply a placeholder within well-rehearsed arguments. The discussion of the strange, al-Qaeda's terrorism, continually risks degenerating into a repetition of the familiar, for instance, a debate on the possibility of the Great Society.

Well-rehearsed arguments are difficult to evaluate in part because they often address real concerns. Poverty does matter. Many people are oppressed by others, or by history, or by circumstance. Energy policy (oil) is important and so are decolonialization, the creation and conduct of Israel, and any number of despotic regimes—not to forget the history of U.S. involvement in the region . . . blood flows, and much has been lost. People have their grievances and their justifications and are in the habit of reciting them at appropriate junctures, but when are such complaints really at the heart of violent darkness? Particularly when one has heard the same thing many times before, one must ask whether the speaker expresses anything beyond a yearning for solidarity.

Even when such arguments are true, they may be practically unimportant. Let us assume, for the moment, the proposition that poverty causes terrorism, a radical oversimplification at best. Considering the durability of poverty, however, what is the consequence of this proposition for security policy? Our efforts to secure ourselves cannot be expected to wait for the elimination of poverty or even the rectification of border issues. In the sweet by and by, of course, security policy will not be necessary, but then, when men are angels, politics will not be necessary either. Until that day, or at least until the construction of a fundamentally better political order, the sort of politics known as security policy will be required.

But the difficulty of thinking more forthrightly about what our enemies represent is not only due to the tendency to take refuge in habitual patterns of thought, nor even just because thinking anew is hard. Thinking about enemies is a psychologically and morally difficult enterprise, especially in this case, in which a hateful intolerance is a real danger. The "Global War on Terror" was a disingenuous phrase but perhaps, therefore, good manners. When the Madrid bombings were blamed on the Basque separatists known as ETA, nobody argued that such people were not capable of terrorist acts. But, we all knew, ETA was not a target of "the war on terror." "Terror," in contemporary parlance, is usually a euphemism for something Islamic, something that is difficult to name without seeming to be an enemy of Islam, and hence of one of the world's great religions and the roughly one billion people, most peaceable and many fellow citizens, who adhere to that faith. Yet even while such divisions are resisted, whether al-Qaeda is understood as "the terrorists" or as the vanguard of the *ummah*, a sense of polarity, of us and them, is palpable. As much as anything else, it is this polarity that makes talk of war unavoidable. But however forgivable the euphemism, in keeping us from naming the enemy in repugnant ways, the word "terror" gives us little purchase on what constitutes the enemy and hinders our understanding of the nature of this conflict.

Not everyone is so squeamish. After 9/11, one began to hear very direct questions about "the" relationship between "Islam" and "violence," as if both concepts were so neatly defined that a single answer could be provided quickly. Some speakers, even nonbelievers, go further and argue that Islam has been hijacked and needs to be "recovered" (how a nonbeliever would go about recovering someone else's religion is difficult to imagine). On the fringes, one hears claims that Islam is inherently terrorist (and in rebuttal, similar claims about the horrors justified by the Bible) or that religion per se is the cause of violence in an otherwise rational world (forgetting the wars fought in the name of Enlightenment). Although primitive and sometimes even ill intentioned, such questions can be steps in the right direction, because they may begin an inquiry into the politics that constitute these wars.

Such inquiry is made difficult, however, by the variety of violent politics with which we are confronted. The security risks and conflicts once addressed under the rubric of the Global War on Terror, and now rather nameless, include a great deal of violence that is conceptually (and often practically) distinct from radical neofundamentalism and particularly from bin Laden's idea of Global Jihad. There is no single description of potential enemies that encompasses U.S. security concerns, even if the discussion is limited to "the Middle East" or "the Muslim world," however such terms might be defined. Much violence is local rather than global. Much violence is motivated by rather old-fashioned nationalism, by tribalism of a seemingly archaic sort, by contemporary reconfigurations of ancient tribes, by solidarity groups smaller than tribes, by banditry, or by explicitly Islamic politics quite different from bin Laden's. And, obviously, these conflicts are not purely Islamist— many of the warriors are not Muslim at all. Consider not just Israel or Lebanon but, of course, the United States itself. Nor are such forms of organization discrete: a warrior's heart may hold multiple, overlapping loyalties, whatever analysts may say. In short, no single paradigm—comparable to the nation for nineteenth-century Europe—adequately describes the politics of the many interrelated conflicts in which we find ourselves engaged.

So how should we start thinking about security in this diffuse context? Let us assume what is quickly becoming received wisdom, that the old ways of understanding threats to our security do not describe many present dangers. In consequence, the models for thinking about containing the threats that were developed over generations when the nation-state was the nearly exclusive form of military organization cannot be presumed to be serviceable and, after nearly a decade of war without much to show, have not in fact served us well. What is to be done?

Encouragingly enough, many people in the security policy community are attempting to engage with the new world, to describe and analyze the new kinds of threats that are presented by the contemporary situation. The military now employs quite a number of anthropologists, experts on religion, and so forth. Books and articles on terrorism, more or less radical Islamic politics, the history of the Middle East, and topics that seem somehow related are proliferating, and many are listed in this book's bibliography. Confronted with the new and strange, we seek to learn, as we should. We turn to experts.

As commendable as such a response is, it is not without its own temptations, for the experts and for the rest of us. Scholarship never ends. We will never completely understand the politics of the Middle East or of Islam for the same reason we never finally understand the politics of the United States or of Christianity. Less objectively but importantly, considerable status and even some money is to be had from being the expert on [my area of expertise, which is really important]. But politics will be done nonetheless, under whatever partial understanding is regnant at the time.

The problems are not merely that politics is intractable and experts are human. The context, government, is inherently difficult. Under the instrumental pressure of policy, thinking is rushed at best and likely to be profoundly biased. Consider the legal opinions on torture, wiretapping, and the like recently offered by a compliant Justice Department.[5] In a modern state in which power is exercised through bureaucracies, inevitably expertise will be used as justification for desired political action. If the expertise is strong, it will be almost impossible to tell, at the time, if the action is justified. Thus, to David Hume's famous aphorism, "[r]eason is, and ought only to be, the slave of the passions," we may add a bureaucratic corollary, "experts are the slaves of politicians."[6]

In a modern government, officials—even elected officials—govern in the name of a rational policy. (This is part of what it means to be an "official," who holds an "office" that provides and limits power; this is part of what it means to be "modern" in the Weberian sense.) The line between official and expert is thin, in part because the office is putatively held on account of merit, much of which is expertise. As a result, the errors of contemporary politics, including security policy, present themselves as intellectual mistakes. It bears repeating, over and over again, that the Vietnam War was in no small part due to "the best and the brightest," and that the NeoCons and even some of the military reformists who have played such prominent roles in our current adventures were also intellectuals. We Americans did not invent hubris and simple folly, but we do express our exercises of power more academically than have other polities.

Knowing the limitations of experts is not to say we can do without them: the only thing worse than officials who think they know everything are officials who do not know anything.

To review the situation, we have new enemies, who need to be understood in order that we may conduct security policy at all. But "enemy," which was once a fairly stable concept, is now a fluid concept—our enemies are determined by affiliation rather than anything so stable as geography or even national citizenship. We turn to experts to understand the new security situation, as we must, but without much hope that the security situation under conditions of globalization can be described with anything like the clarity of international relations founded on the military monopoly of the nation-state, which, come to think of it, was never that clear. Moreover, in turning to experts on the new dangers, we yet again subject ourselves to the limitations inherent in reliance on expertise.

I think this is a fair statement of the contemporary context of security thought. But is this the best we can make of our situation?

No. It is necessary, but not enough, for security policy to be based on a renewed understanding of the world in which it operates. If we are to deploy ourselves responsibly, however, we cannot treat Islamist violence (the GWOT or the Long War) as essentially like the Cold War or like any of our other wars organized by essentially nationalist scripts, with different actors playing the role of bad guys. Such redescriptions are insufficient. The fact of globalization means that we must learn to think about security in a new mode, rather than merely think in the same ways about new enemies. But how do we literally rethink security?

It has become a cliché to say that "the solution" in Afghanistan and Iraq and elsewhere is political, or primarily political, rather than military. Although pleasant-sounding enough and rarely thought through, politics, in fact, does offer us a different way to approach the construction of the global security order. Specifically, this book maintains that we must learn to think about security as an aspect of global politics, in which people everywhere participate and are, in that sense, political actors if not U.S. citizens. To engage the world politically in fact (as opposed to using "political" as a false antithesis to "military," and thereby voicing dissatisfaction with our violence), we must overcome several substantial obstacles to engaging security issues, and especially to threats arising from within the Muslim world, in political terms.

As detailed in the next chapter, we must beware objective description that precludes conversation with others, who are inherently subjects. Conversely, by talking to others, even people who might choose to be our enemies, we not only do politics but we might learn about their politics.[7] So this book proceeds by cabining what might broadly be called economics, history, and sociology (academic techniques for explaining what people really mean, despite what they say) to think about a security policy that engages other people more directly. That is, the argument that follows is essentially and unavoidably subjective, for the simple reason that politics is subjective.

I understand that an essentially subjective understanding of Islamist violence as a threat to our security, and of our security policy in response to that threat, poses substantial difficulties for bureaucratic (policy) analysis, which, after all, claims to be objective, empirical, and the like, rather than subjective, discretionary, and so forth. The modern idea of the bureaucrat, including security policy, is rational—and I am arguing that politics is subjective. While I am sympathetic to the epistemological difficulties of security bureaucrats, I do not think there is an alternative: understanding security in political terms requires a substantial degree of subjective, even sympathetic, reasoning. Perhaps a useful analogy might be made to political campaigns: demographics and other "facts" are important, and the enterprise must be managed by political parties and other bureaucratic institutions, including that of the campaign itself, but the crux of the matter is what do people believe; how are they engaged?

If we can overcome the obstacles to political engagement with Islamist violence, however, we can construct a security policy that others will support, or at least not violently oppose. We can confront Islamist violence more powerfully, more successfully, and with less loss of life than our current approach. Or so it may be hoped.

CHAPTER FIVE

POLITICAL SUBJECTS

Theater is a good metaphor for the situation that we collectively produce and call politics. In thinking politically, as "politically" is used in ordinary speech and in this book, we understand other people, whom we sometimes even call "political actors," to be sharing the same stage with us, whether that stage is called the nation, the polity, or even global society. And like theater, politics cannot be done alone. Politics arises from communication. A political actor, then, is one who is engaged in political communication, on the stage.

There are many actors, so each of us cannot actually speak with all of the others—dialogue is too much to ask—but nonetheless, politics is conducted under the banner of speech and its complement, hearing. For a familiar example, in the context of national politics, we speak of citizens as those entitled to participate in the political process, and to express themselves by voting. Familiar questions are: Who is legally entitled to participate? Are poor people? Members of other races? Women? Much of U.S. history can be understood as the story of how national citizenship has become more inclusive. And in this story, those who were not entitled to vote were not considered political actors. So, in thinking politically, we understand one another to be actors, entitled to participate in the conversation, and thereby to engage in producing a political situation.[1]

One of the principal ideas in this book is that, *after globalization, everyone is a political actor, engaged in making that collective situation we refer to as global society.* This is part of what it means to take globalization seriously. I am not making a utopian statement. I do not mean to suggest that all people, everywhere, are citizens. Although all people, in principle, are entitled to fundamental human rights, that hardly means they enjoy the same entitlements to vote, speak, assemble, or otherwise act politically. And it would be foolish to speak as if all people, in fact, enjoyed the same level of power, however power might be understood. My point is more modest. If the context of political thought, and particularly security thought, is global, then we need to understand that countless actors come together in many different ways, employing economic, military, media, and other discourses, as well as the traditional institutional discourses of politics (e.g., elections), to create global society.

Understanding *everyone* politically, which includes even foreigners and especially enemies, is admittedly difficult. The foreign is by definition strange, outside the realms of the familiar in which we participate. But the problem is not merely, or most essentially, ignorance. If ignorance were the problem, we could simply educate ourselves out of it. We could travel and learn foreign languages and otherwise make familiar what had been foreign and strange. While I enjoy travel, and education is a fine thing, neither, in and of itself, leads to thinking politically.

Consider an act of terrorism, perhaps physicians becoming suicide bombers. Such violence is shocking. People seek explanations. Confronted with such violence, even if they can do nothing about the situation and are only trying to make up their own minds, people ask, "Why?" Leaders of government, with their armies of analysts and planners, often do try to do something about it, that is, understand such a violent act as a problem to be solved and more or less nobly seek a solution. To solve a problem, one might reasonably try to understand the stakes, the mechanisms, the context. And we, the powerful and the powerless alike, should ask why; we should learn all we can, interpret in good faith, and try to understand. We all should, in a word, think critically, and nobody more carefully or critically than public servants, because they are responsible for the consequences of their decisions. (How could I argue otherwise?)

However, there is a real tension between thinking critically and doing politics. In seeking to understand, in explaining conflict in terms of preexisting reasons, we almost necessarily discount the importance of the people involved. Rephrased, in looking for causes in the past, we shift our focus away from our fellow actors, who are with us in the present, looking to the future. But it is our fellow actors with whom we share the world's stage and perform those plays known as politics. Let me make an analogy: Much analysis of U.S. politics in the twentieth century turned on the racism of white voters, especially in the South (e.g., the election of President Nixon). Without denying the existence of racism in the South, once one has explained action in terms of a prior cause, here racism, then the actor in question tends to disappear, and to be understood as merely a symptom of something deeper. And having so decided, we do not have to listen to racists speak, now, because we believe that we already understand what they are really saying, and in fact find it loathsome. We have, in short, decided that the racist is not on our stage, not part of our play. We have disenfranchised him. And perhaps disenfranchising is the right thing to do, in some scheme of things, but it is not doing politics with that Southerner.

There are any number of by-now familiar answers to our demand for explanations for Islamist violence. We have many ways to explain other people objectively, thereby freeing ourselves from having to think of them subjectively, that is, as political subjects, fellow actors. Consider, by way of example, the following.[2]

A SHORT GLOSSARY OF RECEIVED IDEAS

Anti-Semitism. Unrest in the Middle East is caused by the anti-Semitism that lies at the heart of both national governments across the region and Islamist movements. The Grand Mufti of Jerusalem, the Ba'ath party in Iraq, and much of the Egyptian elite were Nazi sympathizers. Since the establishment of Israel, anti-Semites across the region have openly called for its elimination. See also *Zionism.*

Christianity. See *Islam.*

Crime. The attacks on the World Trade Center and other acts of terrorism are essentially the work of criminals, for which the proper response is police action. Bin Laden and other criminals do not represent a state, and therefore this is not a war. Calling the terrorist situation a war is merely convenient for the governments of the United States, Great Britain, and other nations, because it allows an expansion of the power of the state.

Crusade. The United States–led wars in Afghanistan and Iraq and the so-called Global War on Terror are merely contemporary expressions of the crusading impulse, the ancient Christian tendency to invade Muslim lands. Before his handlers got to him, President Bush even said, plainly, that this was a crusade. And what about the abuse and repression of Muslims in European nations—is that any different from the repression of Muslims under the Spanish "reconquest"? See also *jihad*.

Democracy/human rights. The chronic instability in the Middle East is due to the failure to establish modern, democratic states that respect human rights. People in the Middle East, like people everywhere, want to be free and to live in dignity, under the law.

Empire. The instability of the Middle East is due to the illegitimate rule by Great Powers, and the understandable efforts of the people to resist such foreign domination. The United States is heir to the colonial mantle of the French and the British.

Freedom. Terrorists hate us because we are free.

Globalization. The structure of contemporary capitalist repression and Western cultural imperialism against which jihad and other forms of rebellion must be waged. See also *nationalism*.

History. The chronic instability of the Middle East is caused by the failure of the Muslim world to continue progressing at about the time that Europe was entering the modern period. Muslims are both ashamed and angry that they have fallen so far behind.

Islam. See *Christianity*.

Jihad. The Muslim tendency to spread Islam by the sword. See also *crusade*.

Nationalism. The chronic instability of the Middle East, like that of the Balkans, is caused by ethnic nationalism. In all but a few instances, the Middle East has failed to establish truly modern states that could accommodate different nationalities.

Oil (1). The chronic instability of the Middle East is caused by the desire of first-world nations, especially the United States, to secure petroleum at a low price. This was announced as the Carter doctrine—the United States would not tolerate threats to its oil supply.

Oil (2). The chronic instability of the Middle East is caused by the corrupting influence of oil-money, which underwrites tyranny, and especially war.

Respect. Terrorists hate us because we do not respect their cultures.

Return of the repressed. The violence of the Muslim world is caused by a backlash against modernization, most obviously illustrated by the fall of the Shah of Iran.

Rulers. The chronic instability of the Middle East is caused by the ambitions of individual men, mostly the rulers of states. For example, President G.W. Bush went to war in Iraq because President Saddam Hussein had attempted to have his father, President H.W. Bush, assassinated. For another example, President G.W. Bush went to war in Iraq to prove to his father, President H.W. Bush, that he, G.W., was tough.

Tribe. This part of the world is essentially tribal, and tribalism organizes—indeed demands—violence.

Weapons of mass destruction. The invasion of Iraq was necessary to ensure that Iraq did not have WMD.

Women (1). The violence, instability, and outright rage of the Muslim World is due to the fact that women are oppressed by a patriarchal society that denies them basic rights.

Women (2). The violence, instability, and outright rage of the Muslim World is due to the fact that men are sexually frustrated.

Women (3). The West attempts to use sex and other temptations as a way to destroy all the cultures of the world, including those of the Middle East, and replace indigenous cultures with a shallow and degrading consumerism, along with the drugs, prostitution, crime, and despair so familiar in Western societies. The Muslim world rebels against this, usually by wearing modest clothing (the veil) but sometimes violently.

Zionism. Unrest in the Middle East is caused by the racist imperialism that lies at the heart of the Israeli government. See also *anti-Semitism*.

One could go on, but there is no need: the point is that much of our thinking about Islamist violence is done through a number of very clichéd ideas. After all, a great "many people think they are thinking when they are merely rearranging their prejudices," as William James famously said. The "thoughts" resulting from such a process are generally unearned, inadequately related to one another, and simply unhelpful. This is unfortunate, and we should try harder.

That said, clichéd thought is inevitable in political discourse. If we talk a lot, we will repeat ourselves, oversimplify. And we cannot learn everything from scratch; we must take much on faith, and so forth and so on. Political speech is messy. Moreover, such clichés, even prejudices, sometimes may be true, or true enough. An idea is not wrong just because it is a cliché, that is, because lots of people repeat it. Nor is an idea wrong just because it is a prejudice, unsupported by independent judgment. So, for examples, the propositions that "it ("it" is usually unspecified, but some part of this mess in the Middle East, with terrorism, etc.) is all about [empire, history (everybody has one), Islam, Israel, oil, tribes, weapons of mass destruction, and so on]" all contain or at least suggest important and relevant truths. There is a great deal to be said, and much of it has been said before, often but not always for less-than-worthy reasons.

As suggested, however, such clichéd explanations tend to be less helpful than one might hope, even when they are in some important sense correct. Such explanations are usually presented as *keys*. Once you understand [this key concept], you will understand the other aspects of the security situation. But such explanations are almost never keys. What was presented as a key, a solution, turns out to be complicated, another problem. The mysteries the key was supposed to unlock simply do not solve themselves. Let me make an analogy: Freudian thought has often been reduced to the proposition that "it's all about sex." Certainly sex is important, and in our everyday lives, we thoughtlessly assume that we know what sex is, but upon a moment's reflection on our own experience, it becomes pretty clear that even sex isn't all about sex. In fact, what we mean by "sex" is far from obvious and certainly not agreed upon in any politically useful sense.[3] For example, much advertising is clearly about sex but also about language, multiple markets, graphic understandings, and so on—none of which can be divorced from the erotic. Once the sexual is understood to permeate the social, then what had seemed so clear, the concept of "sex," loses much of its explanatory force. Similarly, once we understand that Islam, Israel, oil, weapons, and so forth all matter very much and cannot be understood apart from one another, then such ideas tend to become considerations, aspects of our thought, but not explanations or keys and certainly not solutions.

Like the trope of the Southern racist, clichéd explanations of what is wrong in Iraq, or why people become terrorists, or what Israel should/ should not do can all too easily become oversimplifications of a complex political environment. Such simplifications are almost always relevant or else they would not have such appeal, but "we know that" can prevent real thinking and, in communities of experts, often does. Precisely because they are partially true, something of a solution, simplifications tend to end inquiry, shut down thought, prematurely. For pertinent example, it is becoming general wisdom that a political solution is necessary in many conflicts—but the uncontroversial consensus that political solutions are to be preferred to military solutions is making it difficult to think through what might be meant by "political" in this context.

Economists, in particular, are fond of defending their failures and over-sights by arguing that simplifications, assumptions, and models are necessary tools for thought and that thinking advances through the progressive refine-ment of such tools. There is truth in this idea, as well as defensiveness and physics envy. At the same time, in some situations, the idea is flat wrong. There are many things that nobody should try to understand as problems that may be modeled and to which solutions may be proposed. *Hamlet* is not a problem to be solved but instead is a situation to be acted through by the players and appreciated—a complex enterprise—by the audience. To under-stand *Hamlet* as "really" or "basically" about something else is not to under-stand *Hamlet* at all, though it may be to understand the something else. Similarly, to understand a contemporary political situation as "really" about anti-Semitism or Zionism is almost inevitably to substitute a clichéd objec-tification for thought.

Although the intellectual problems raised by simplification are impor-tant, we should remember that most such simplifications are not, at bottom, intended for intellectual use. To say that simplification of a security situation fails intellectually is to presume that the primary purpose of such simpli-fication is intellectual, which is rarely if ever the case. (Really, I've thought about it. It is all about Israel. Isn't that interesting?) The simplifications that pervade public discourse and inform policy argument generally have polit-ical, rather than intellectual, purposes. So what are the *political* problems with our oversimplifications?

As already suggested, not only ideologies, clichéd explanations, and prej-udices but the most thoughtful analysis can objectify people, so that they become causes of the problem and cease to be actors, and politics comes to an end. Objective analysis, precisely because it is objective, tends to exclude the subjectivity that is inherent in the doing of politics. The "is" of cultural analysis, however sophisticated, does not become the "ought" of normative thought, still less the "let's" of political action, without human intervention. And it is among these all-too-human interventions, when people are making up their minds about what to do, that politics occurs. Thus, in thinking *about* a situation (an intellectual problem), we almost inevitably exclude others, and for that matter ourselves, from discourse (a political problem). Sometimes this is correct; politics is not always possible. But sometimes we should insist on doing politics, on letting conversation trump representa-tion, participation trump precision.

At issue is the scope of political participation. Simplifications, and especially "arguments" for the simplifications, serve to unify the faithful, express the essentially political yearning for solidarity. In preaching to the choir, we demonstrate our belief and strengthen it in each other and in ourselves. Thus, if we are convinced that the choir includes everyone that we care about, we may simplify the world outside to the choir's, to our heart's content. So, among Zionists, one may speak of anti-Semitism; among jihadists, of the Great Satan; and so forth, but the difficulty for the United States is that, in order for its global security order to work, the appeal of that order must be very broad indeed.

Insidiously, and even when we are at our most idealistic, our need to understand the foreign and dangerous contexts in which globalized security policy is conducted presents another kind of difficulty for the responsible conceptualization of U.S. policy. When analysis is sophisticated, perhaps particularly when it is sophisticated, working so hard to understand the unfamiliar and even unknown tends to take our minds off of ourselves. In a word, we are tempted to take our intentions, our plans, and especially our institutions for granted. We are apt to lose the capacity for self-criticism precisely when our intentions are best.

But the failures of the last few years, and the emergence of the postwar context, make it clear that our intentions, plans, and institutions cannot be taken for granted, but instead should be subject to serious reconsideration. At the present juncture, it is not enough to ask the classic question, what is to be done? If the United States is to exercise force responsibly, we cannot avoid asking what are *we* to do, and are *we* equipped to do it?

This book argues that U.S. security policy, especially including policy on Islamist violence, can be organized through a deeper conception of what doing politics requires. Security politics extends over global space, and therefore the first conceptual task, undertaken by this chapter, is to reimagine the foreigner, even the enemy, hitherto outside of (domestic) politics, as a fellow political subject, if not a citizen. Doing so requires us to resist, on a regular basis, the tendency of critical analysis to objectify, and hence banish our fellow actors from the global stage.

CHAPTER SIX

POLITICS IS NOW

We Americans traditionally have thought of the appearance of our republic as something of significance not just to those of us who live here but to humanity. We have believed ourselves—do believe ourselves—to be at the forefront of History. This is not exclusively American, of course: revolutionaries always claim to be writing History, and Enlightenment thinkers generally have thought that "progress" would make most traditional human arrangements obsolete. While the American heritage has both revolutionary and Enlightened aspects, so does the heritage of other nations, for obvious example, France. And there are other ways for polities to believe themselves of universal importance: consider the Jews, God's chosen people; or the Arab expansion; or the Chinese—many people in many times have believed that they were making History in the grandest of senses, and sometimes they were right. Nonetheless, for present purposes it is important to realize that the American belief in the historical importance, even necessity, of the United States is a powerful thing, and critical to understanding the nation's foreign policy.

Implicit in this notion—call it "American modernism" because it fuses the national and the historical—is a corollary belief, now rarely made explicit, that the way the United States does things now is the way other countries will do things soon. To be blunt, our linear and progressive view of history carries with it a certain disdain for other societies, and other peoples, perceived as less modern, even premodern. To exaggerate for the sake of clarity, Americans are usually too polite to make clear their belief that, in

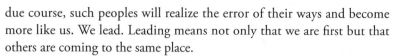

due course, such peoples will realize the error of their ways and become more like us. We lead. Leading means not only that we are first but that others are coming to the same place.

American modernism tends to constrict American judgment. Since the United States expresses the historical narrative that matters, the narratives of other peoples are hardly of interest. As a result, the political significance of U.S. actions is to be determined vis-à-vis the American narrative. We understand what we have done because we understand the history, our own history, against which our actions are to be judged. Thus our understanding of history hinders our efforts to understand the significance of our violence in other's eyes. After all, it is often said, they stopped developing in the fourteenth century. Something, to quote a famous book, "went wrong" in the Islamic world, and historical progress slowed to a crawl.[1] Muslims were left, and in important ways have remained, in an essentially "medieval" state.

It bears remembering that the word "medieval"—the middle age—was coined as a counterweight in a time when many people self-consciously spoke of a renaissance, a rebirth of ancient learning and classical virtues. If what soon enough came to be called "the Renaissance" defined itself as a time of rediscovery, then logically there were times during which the accomplishments of the Greeks and Romans were forgotten or ignored, the so-called "Middle Ages." Of course, people in the Middle Ages did not think of themselves in those terms; they thought they were living now. And today, as a matter of historical judgment, it is not at all clear when the Middle Ages should be said to have begun or ended, so that the Renaissance could be said to have begun. Such questions are interesting, and as an intellectual matter, dividing time into periods may be necessary in order that we may categorize, analyze, and otherwise discuss the succession of changes and continuities we call history.

At the same time, however, we should remember that such periods, and indeed the more or less objective description of history, is a way of thinking about societies—including politics—in time. But such thinking is somewhat academic or at least contemplative and cannot be the workaday perspective of those who are actually doing politics. If we examine the practice of even the most radical, or "archaic," Islamist political groups, we find a great deal of positioning, alliances, scheming, cajoling, renewal, and dissolution—the sorts of striving that we would expect of any political party.[2] Like others with intense political aspirations, in all sorts of ways, radical Islamists appear to live very much in the present. Muslims, even terrorists, are also our contemporaries. We are all on stage.

To understand politics as conversation or discourse is more than metaphorical. Emphasizing the conversational nature of politics highlights its temporality: conversation occurs right now. Indeed, when someone is only a little ahead of us (usually interrupting or otherwise impatient), we tend to find it rude, or at least, not a conversation. Worse, when someone is slow. . . . Thus, in doing politics, each of us acknowledges the presence of others, the people we are trying to persuade or elect or whose authority we acknowledge—the others who, with us, compose the political action. Therefore, if we are serious about understanding security in terms of politics, if we believe Clausewitz's proposition that war is a form of politics, and if politics is always in the present tense, then *we must understand our fellow members of global society, even our Islamist enemies, in the present tense, as our contemporaries, with whom we converse, however angrily at times.*

Thinking politically thus entails an imagination of time. In doing politics, we presume certain things about time and related concepts like history and the future. Unfortunately for present purposes, the temporality of political discourse is at odds with the American modernism we so often employ to confront the world in general, and the Muslim world in particular. For simple and important example, it is difficult to dismiss somebody as medieval and also take him seriously as a political interlocutor. The medieval era is past; politics is about the contemporary struggle for the shape of tomorrow. As a result of this temporal mismatch, it is difficult for many Americans to think about doing politics in a medieval context, in much the same way that objective explanations ("he thinks like this because he hates Jews") can make political discourse impossible. If we wish to do politics in the world of Islam, we must learn how to bracket if not abandon some of our own historical narratives, so that we understand that, at least for political purposes, we are not only on the same stage, we are there at the same time.

But while we might acknowledge the logical or abstract necessity of understanding Muslims, even the Taliban or al-Qaeda, as our contemporaries, it is difficult for many Americans to *feel* that Islamist politics are contemporary. We are very used to understanding practices that we abhor—the radical subjugation of women, for example—in terms of a historical narrative in which our values triumphantly inherit the future, and the values we oppose die. Words like "medieval," "archaic," or "tribal" are difficult to get around.

The risk of such conceptions, though, is that we banish Muslims who are insufficiently like us to the past, and politics is not begun.

Consider the following somewhat notorious statement:

> "The clash we are witnessing around the world is not a clash of religions or a clash of civilizations," Dr. Sultan said. "It is a clash between two opposites, between two eras. It is a clash between a mentality that belongs to the Middle Ages and another mentality that belongs to the twenty-first century. It is a clash between civilization and backwardness, between the civilized and the primitive, between barbarity and rationality."[3]

So spoke Wafa Sultan, a Syrian American medical doctor living outside Los Angeles. Sultan's statements, broadcast on al Jazeera, provoked death threats; her interviews have been downloaded millions of times; and the excitement itself became a media event. What makes Sultan's statement notable is not its content but its impolitic candor. In her view, Islamist terrorism is a battle against the course of history, albeit history understood in a particular way. We may call this understanding of history "Enlightened History," and this understanding of terrorism "the return of the repressed."

Muslims and secularists like Sultan and perhaps most Americans respond to Enlightened History in very different ways. To be more specific, in their debates over "the Muslim question," contemporary Muslims, especially in the West, and Western secularists in the United States and elsewhere take very different stances toward history, and much of the contemporary "clash" between "Islam" and "the West" can be understood as expressions of widespread anxieties over history.

Perhaps surprisingly, this is a good thing, for two reasons. First, our imaginations of history can be talked over, even changed, with relatively little of the existential drama so often found in arguments over civilization or religion. And second, if we are to do politics in serious fashion, a historical perspective can never be far away. What kind of history do we wish to leave our children? How will we, in our turn, be judged?

Of course there are many different ways to be a Muslim, or a Westerner, or sometimes a Muslim in the West, or a Westerner among Muslims. In such confusing situations, law professors often "clarify" matters by posing hypotheticals, little stories that use individuals to facilitate the exploration of more general legal principles. Sometimes, we flatteringly remind ourselves that Plato did something similar in his dialogues. So, for the purposes of theoretical exploration, let us represent these two stances toward "Enlightened History" through two characters, each of whom is a middlebrow intellectual working in good faith, Jamal and John.

How many people, and with what degrees of variation, subscribe to these positions? I do not know and doubt one could have precise sociological knowledge about something as ineffable as the imagination of history entwined in the assumption of political stances. But whatever precision of knowledge about the intersection of the social and the imaginary is possible, we need not ascertain the demographics of souls in order to explore structures of belief.

John believes in Enlightened History, believes that humanity is progressing from primitive backwardness to civilization, from barbarism to rationality. Enlightened History is like a cable, braided from many wires, stretching from the past to the future, from the primitive to the civilized. Moving along any one wire will take one in the direction of all the other wires, in the direction of the cable as a whole, toward the modern, which is much the same thing as the future. After all, John reasons, we can identify some politics as progressive, because they represent progress toward modernity.

The outlines of Enlightened History are familiar. History is a process of secularization, both of thought and of social life. Faith gives way to reason, especially science, and therefore, religious practices and institutions decline. The Middle Ages, the age of hierarchy founded on status and oath, gives way to modern equality before the rational laws of the nation-state. Community and tradition are replaced by individualism and enterprise. The king, aristocracy, and peasantry are replaced by a democratic bourgeoisie and a laboring class. Most of this was made explicit in the French Revolution, in which the French executed their king and declared an atheistic government. Although the French Revolution's excesses engendered a partial counterrevolution, the state came to see itself as a secularizing institution, responsible for improving the well-being of its citizens, well-being that was and is understood in bourgeois terms of material comfort and secure social position— thus the course of history according to John.

Enlightened History is deeply offensive to Jamal for at least five related reasons. First, regardless of which strand of wire in the cable one chooses, his country has failed to progress very far in the direction of what John calls modern. Enlightened History is a none-too-subtle way of calling Jamal's world backward.

Second, Jamal knows how this movie ends: the medieval is superseded by the modern. From the perspective of Enlightened History, everything that Jamal believes in will be wrapped up in a ball labeled "culture," "religion," and "medieval," all of which will be thrown out on the ash heap, to use the image of another big believer in Enlightened History, Marx.

Third, Enlightened History suggests not just that Jamal's religion, Islam, will like all religions go away, but that Islam should be understood in historical, rather than holy, terms. John insinuates that Jamal's God is no God, and that Jamal's belief in a God is a mere function of his position in human history. Thus Enlightened History seems to be an aggressive form of atheism.

Fourth and more subtly, Jamal comes to understand Enlightened History less as a form of atheism and more as a rival religion. John *believes* in Enlightened History, believes in the collective human progress away from faith and toward a free-standing rationality; that is, he believes in secularism.[4] This belief is sustained in spite of a great deal of evidence to the contrary provided by the events of the last 200 years or so. After all, the French Revolution ended in bloody tyranny. That preacher of Enlightened liberty Jefferson held slaves, and our constitutional republic slaughtered its own over the privilege. By similar token, rationalist Europe was also colonial Europe. Trench warfare, the Holocaust, fire, and then nuclear bombing (an American specialty), to say nothing of putting the survival of humanity into play during the Cold War and genocides ignored—this is the unfolding of rationality? Turning from history to epistemology, Western thinkers have, in the course of the nineteenth and twentieth centuries, been rather hard on the idea that rationality is easily achieved and underlies our politics. And if we turn to society, it is difficult to see this alleged rationality. Western societies seem to be structured by irrational interests, fashion, and lusts leading to prisons, drugs, environmental degradation (perhaps catastrophic), and so forth.

Finally, Jamal might note that Enlightened History is not unlike Christian history, marching toward a time of redemption. In fact, this mirroring of Christian history in secular terms is explicit in Hegel and implicit in Marx—one of the reasons we can speak of the fall of communism in terms of the God that failed. But surely the Marxists were just more forthright than contemporary American secular humanists about their effort to make

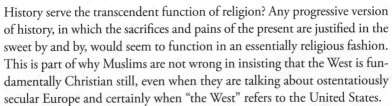

History serve the transcendent function of religion? Any progressive version of history, in which the sacrifices and pains of the present are justified in the sweet by and by, would seem to function in an essentially religious fashion. This is part of why Muslims are not wrong in insisting that the West is fundamentally Christian still, even when they are talking about ostentatiously secular Europe and certainly when "the West" refers to the United States.

If he were intellectually sensitive, John might understand that Jamal finds Enlightened History an offensive philosophy. But John actually understands the world in terms of Enlightened History. Despite whatever etiquette might require (usually a change of topic), John understands Jamal to be inescapably and futilely angry at history itself. Indeed, John may even sympathize, in subtly patronizing fashion: certainly colonialism, and many of the despotic regimes established in its wake, were horrible things. And from the Muslim perspective, John reasons, the process just continues. Muslim cultures are being transformed, being assimilated, and will fade away. No wonder so many Muslims are so angry, and no wonder some hotheads become terrorists. With a bow toward Freud, John understands terrorism as the return of the repressed, a violent response to a modernization that has gone too fast. With this move, John deploys Enlightened History to provide psychological (and collectively, political) reassurance that Islamist terrorism is rage against the course of modernity and, in the long view, a passing thing.

However comforting, understanding terrorism as the return of the repressed should not be entirely convincing, even to John. The problem is that John has his own doubts about Enlightened History. Religion does not seem to be going away. History may be progressing, but it does not seem to be progressing toward a secular future very quickly, if at all. Millions upon millions actively believe. Instead of replacing religion, as planned, politics is increasingly waged in religious terms, not only in places where political Islam is a force but in the United States. And insofar as modern society is structured by markets, which it clearly is, modernity is imbued with the irrationality of markets, manias and losses of confidence, fashion and herd behavior, pervasive corruption, and data without meaning that cannot be squared with "rational."

Although John is not sure that he still believes in Enlightened History, Jamal is hardly confident in his denial of Enlightened History. The countries that claim to be modern have achieved a great deal, in virtually every area of life. Therefore, when the West claims to represent the future, Jamal finds it hard not to be impressed, to some degree persuaded. Moreover, Jamal also tends to consider history in linear terms; Jamal dates time from the Prophet. And Jamal knows that during the Christian Middle Ages, Muslim countries were in many respects more "advanced"—it is hard to find another word— than the countries of Western Europe. If he is candid, Jamal may admit that some aspects of Islam, or at least contemporary Islamic practice, look backward in time and restrict innovation, and hence adaptation to the contemporary world. Jamal may call for a reform, probably including an opening of the door of *ijtihad* (reinterpretation of the tradition). Jamal may argue for historicization of the Islamic tradition (those things were done then, under different circumstances). Perhaps Jamal will call for a reformation equivalent to Luther's, which is widely held to have ended the (Christian) Middle Ages and begun the modern era in the West.[5] But by this point, Jamal will have come perilously close to adopting the conceptual structure of Enlightened History, which, as we have seen, he is at pains to deny.

Thus we have American secularists like John, committed to the truth of Enlightened History but concerned that it may be false, and we have Muslims like Jamal, who must deny Enlightened History but are worried that it may be true.

Discussions of Islamist conflicts tend to be framed, often implicitly, by "the Muslim question."[6] Is a reform, or at least a "reformulation," of Islam necessary for the modern world? Consider the possibility, however, that at least as good a question concerns the frame of the frame, that is, the Western modernity in which the Muslim question is asked. Perhaps Jamal's objections to, and John's doubts about, the belief that history is a monolithic process of rational secularization are right. In that case, one might ask, does the West need a reformulation of its historical imagination in order to be compatible with what it has become, including Muslim? I think so.

The possibility that Enlightened History will cease to be credible is the half-articulated preoccupation running through a great deal of American (and French) public discourse. Certainly the rational does not appear to be overcoming the religious, even in the most "advanced" countries. Many Americans, and perforce politicians, are quite religious. At the same time, and to some large degree in response (the Darwinist car-bumper mockery of the Christian fish springs to mind, as does the French hysteria over clothing), we are seeing the revival of, pardon the oxymoron, an enthusiastic atheism. An environmental asceticism, lent urgency by the universal guilt of global warming, is imposing itself on our discourse and habits. The substance of such beliefs, still less the spiritual and intellectual characters of the believers, is not at issue here beyond this: rather than the long-awaited (since at least Voltaire) decline of religion, we observe the proliferation of all sorts of religious spirit. We may, with Olivier Roy, go a step further and note that our process of globalization has been accompanied by a general rise in religiosity, that is, religious feelings that are decoupled from the continuities of time and place that used to be called culture.[7]

In passing, let me suggest that the concept of "the modern" may be unraveling for us, or more precisely, we may be recalling the old truth that every age has its experience of change, and its own sense of "the modern." It bears remembering that the English word was used in the late 1400s, and the contrast between ancient and modern was easy for Thucydides.[8] But for much of the late nineteenth and most of the twentieth centuries the modern appeared to be something more specific, an essentially unified process (rationalization, mechanization, liberation, and so forth), and that inchoate but self-confident conception of the world now seems to be fragmenting. "The modern"—or, at least, what's next—now appears to be far more fragmented, disorganized, and even self-contradictory. Rather than the replacement of culture and tradition by a rationalistic modernity, we also find new associations formed in the context of a fluid global society, new ways of being together, many of which, from capitalism to religiosity to new nationalisms to bureaucratic accommodations to social networking, are less than rational but no less human or contemporary. To cope with this confusing situation, each of us continually employs various, and conflicting, conceptions of what it is to be modern.[9]

The decline of Enlightened History as a dominant paradigm would be salutary for the politics of Muslims, both abroad and here in the United States, in at least two ways. First, if they can escape from the conceptual framework of Enlightened History, Muslims need not defend themselves from the claim that they are, by virtue of their beliefs, historically retrograde. Less defensiveness may facilitate Muslim political discourse by transforming the embarrassing question "how do we become modern?" into the less-charged language of ordinary politics, "what is to be done?"

Second, as already mentioned, notions of history are more accessible than tenets of faith. Muslims and others have found themselves arguing for an Islamic reformation. But while religious movements usually involve argument, changes in faith are rarely summoned by argument (although Luther's 95 theses come close). Calling for a reformation is like calling for a prophet; much more than argument is at work. Thus, an enormous gulf exists between Muslim arguments that "Islam needs a reformation" in order to become "modern" and actually experiencing the transformation and renewal of faith that constitute religious reformation. In contrast, imaginations of history are relatively amenable to argument. Nothing in the Islamic tradition requires Muslims to understand history in tripartite fashion and to relegate themselves to the second era, now past, awaiting a reformation so that they can recapitulate the history of Western Europe, as decisively important as that history has been to humans everywhere.

Moreover, if we abandon—or at least bracket—the idea that history has a single direction, we may begin to understand the contemporary appeal of al-Qaeda and radical neofundamentalism more generally. This will be argued in more detail in the next chapter, but briefly, neofundamentalism is not the expression of the culture of any given time or place but instead a stripping down of religious life, complexly situated, to a code, which can be translated, replicated, and transported. Islamic associations, including al-Qaeda, may be thoroughly modern in their processes of adherence and transmission, even if their strictures often seem anachronistic to Westerners. Thus the modernity of Muslims is not turning out as Enlightened History would predict (this, in brief, was the Neoconservative error). Nor should we dismiss the violence of radical neofundamentalism, however repugnant, as the return of the repressed, that is, as belonging to an earlier time, a form of misbehavior that we have, through historical progress, transcended. Not only have we "moderns" committed our own barbarisms but also the radical neofundamentalists are our contemporaries. Even al-Qaeda should be understood as an essentially contemporary phenomenon, imaginable in its present form only after the successes, and failures, of the modern history of political Islam. Radical neofundamentalism represents an all-too-plausible modernity and needs to be confronted on that basis, a project that the next chapters undertake.

But more than misunderstanding our enemies is at stake, as dangerous as misunderstanding an enemy can be. Americans need to understand, and limit, their claims to operate under the mandate of History. It is odd that this point still needs to be made—this, if nothing else, we should have learned from the Soviet and German disasters. As the epigraph to this book has it, nations are punished for their transgressions. And there is no greater temptation to transgression than being convinced that actions are required by the course of History. (Isn't that right, Macbeth?)

More affirmatively, if we are to do politics globally—and politics includes questions of security—then we should recognize that we are speaking in the present tense. History is never absent—as Faulkner said of the past, it's not even passed—but political discourse presumes the construction, right now, with the resources available to us, of our collective future.[10] We are in the present tense, and moving forward, together. Thus these ugly conflicts, despite their horrors, present opportunities for all sides to realize that they already are modern. The mostly intellectual difficulty that we confront is that "modern" is not what we have long thought, nor can it yet be articulated easily. Indeed, by definition the modern is something that we work on, construct, together, and at least as a matter of politics rather than revelation, we cannot know how it will play out.

CHAPTER SEVEN

THE MODERNISM OF RADICAL
NEOFUNDAMENTALISM

Announcements of terrorist acts are often met with surprise, which gradually gives way to mystification. How could anyone teach the young—the hope of the future—to kill themselves? How could engineers do anything so manifestly irrational—to say nothing of evil—as fly a plane into an office building? How could doctors attack an airport?

Our mystification does not arise out of a vacuum. To be mystified is to realize that we do not, in fact, understand what we thought we knew. The mystification with which we confront the 9/11 attacks, and so much contemporary terrorism, therefore tells us something about how we have been thinking, that is, tells us about our tacit assumptions. Many of these assumptions have to do with how history and related ideas, like rationality, religion, culture, and progress, works, that is, assumptions about what makes the modern world modern. Such understandings tend to be vague, commonly held, and rather unconsidered. Until assumptions are upset, perhaps because we are shocked by terrorism, we may not consciously realize what we think, and because our thinking is unexamined, we have little idea of how right, or how wrong, our thinking is. "It does not make sense" is a very human and correct response, at least initially.

Chapter Five argued that many familiar assumptions about Islamist violence only appear to offer solutions but, in fact, tend to make political discourse, and therefore real solutions, less likely. Chapter Six argued that our conceptions of history, especially our ideas about who is and who is not "modern," should not blind us to the fact that politics requires speaking and listening in the present tense. This chapter asserts that many assumptions about the causes of terrorist violence, and more conversely, about the nature of the modern, are simply misleading because they do not fit the facts of the terrorist attacks that today seem most significant, including the 9/11 attacks.

There are, of course, apologists for terrorists, who argue that we can, in fact, understand contemporary terrorism in terms of familiar, indeed ortho-dox, stories. The most familiar such explanation holds that terrorism is a ra-tional or at least understandable effort by people without good weapons to seek liberation under the motto "one man's terrorist is another man's free-dom fighter." But while this and similar commonplace explanations may address some terrorism in some times and places, such apologetic explana-tions are politically useless (Chapter Five) and moreover, do not account for much contemporary terrorism.[1] If we realize the insufficiency of such apolo-gies for terrorism, however, we are left without an appropriate story to tell and so are not only outraged by terrorist violence but genuinely and cor-rectly mystified—back where we started.

How could bin Laden be modern? One way bin Laden is modern is through military innovation; nothing tactically like 9/11 had ever been achieved before. On the level of ideas, too, Global Jihad is different in kind from conflict as imagined by Clausewitz or others who seek to explain war as an instrument of the state, including those who understand this war sim-ply negatively (and ethnocentrically) as the consequence of misbegotten policies of the United States and other mostly Western powers. Nor can Global Jihad be conceptualized in tribal or traditional terms. Nor, as dis-cussed below, can Global Jihad be understood within traditional Islamic thought (though it cannot be understood without traditional Islamic thought, either). Bin Laden and other radical neofundamentalists have pre-sented us with a new and unfamiliar kind of politics, and hence of war, and appreciating these differences is a prerequisite to an informed policy.

Some understanding of what is new here requires some attention to what is old; appreciation of what is innovative and even deeply modern about the contemporary conflict requires some knowledge of tradition through and against which this "modern" is defined. Specifically, to understand what makes bin Laden's politics, and hence his war, so radical, it is helpful to sketch four different understandings of the relationship between Islam and political life, including warfare, that have been widely held among Muslims: (1) the Islamic politics of the Prophet and the right-guided caliphs, (2) the diffident and somewhat judgmental relationship between Islamic discourse and everyday political life in the Muslim tradition stretching from shortly after the days of the Prophet to the present, (3) the political Islam that arose in the twentieth century, and (4) the contemporary, even postmodern, neofundamentalism that has emerged in recent years.[2] Taken together, these four conceptions of political life compose a tradition, albeit a highly contested one. Radical neofundamentalism must be understood as an outgrowth of this tradition, but as we will see in Chapter Eight, it also represents a substantial rupture.[3]

The First Understanding: The Time of the Prophet

The Prophet, his companions, and his immediate successors are believed to have conducted political life in perfect accordance with the law (*sharia*). Sunnis, Twelver Shi'ites, and Ismailis disagree on which successors, and so how long this period lasts, but all believe that accounts of the actions of the Prophet and his companions (*hadith*), including political actions, are both sources of and guides to the nature of the law. In the same vein, the *ummah* is said (at least by Sunnis) to be incapable of making a mistake. Thus, with regard to the very early days, it makes little sense to speak of a relationship *between* Islam and political life, that is, to understand one as separable from the other. Islam encompassed political life; political life exemplified Islam.

The Second Understanding: Rulers and Scholars

For those who are not the Prophet or immediately connected to him, that is, people who have lived in the ensuing centuries, the relationship between politics and Islam is much less clear. Islam is believed to inform all aspects of right living, and *sharia* is perfect, eternal. Politics, in the sense of ruling or administration, in contrast, is essentially bound in time. Those in authority must make practical decisions, often based on imperfect information and in bad circumstances. While such political decisions (*siyasa*) have the force of law, they cannot claim to have the authority of *the* law, *sharia*.

Traditionally, then, Muslim societies exhibit a tension akin to the Western tension between positive law (the will of the ruler, especially as embodied in legal texts) and justice (as determined by God, nature, or morality). This tension may be reflected in the structure of Muslim societies, in which different authorities rely on different aspects of the law. The ruler has his officials, whose actions constitute *siyasa*. *Ulema*, scholars of Islamic law who are also judges (*qadis*), rule in accordance with *sharia*. Ideally, each respects the authority of the other. Officials do not contravene *sharia* and may even consult *ulema*. But *ulema* have no power to set policy or otherwise bind the government, although they may condemn bad acts committed by the government. Instead, the *ulema* must hope that the ruler is a good Muslim. The language of politics is, at the end of the day, not the clearest language of God. (Analogies in the West may be found in Augustinian and Lutheran traditions of political thought, with their insistence on the incomplete nature of political life, and in the strong distinction between policy and law.)

One should not overdo this distinction between official and *ulema*. The issue is contested, but nothing so absolute as a distinction between politics and religion, or separation between the state and the church, need be implied. In many Muslim societies, Islam permeates life, including political and so military life. In wars with the infidel, an explicitly Islamic discourse may prevail. For example, the Ottoman Empire's struggle with the Allies in World War I was characterized as a jihad, a holy war. Moreover, within Muslim societies, calls for reform—efforts to make society more Islamic—have occurred throughout history, most famously the *salafi* movement that began with al Wahhab in the eighteenth century. Such reform efforts have often been "fundamentalist" in character, that is, they have insisted on the primacy of the Koran and the ways of the Prophet and were antagonistic to accretions of culture and tradition in the intervening years. Albeit in ways very different from the fundamentalist reformers, the mystical Sufi movements also sought to imbue everyday life with a greater sense of religious moment and, in doing so, to dissolve the bounds between the transcendent and the banal.

While wars, fundamentalist reforms, and mystical movements from time to time affirmed the Islamic nature of all human life, including politics, the very extraordinary nature of such developments testifies to the status quo normal, in which policy and the institutions of administrative governance, on the one hand, are readily distinguishable from less worldly forms of life, including scholarship and the judiciary, on the other hand. Asked explicitly,

Muslims might deny any distinction between Islam and politics, and hence any distinction between church and state on the Western model. This is true, in its way, but as already suggested, a simplification somewhat likely to mislead. If all authority is ultimately from God, then no area can simultaneously claim to be ungodly and authoritative. So Muslim rulers rule in the name of Islam, because no other form of rule is Islamically authoritative. That said, the distinctions between policy and law, *siyasa* and *sharia*, administration and judiciary, temporal power and atemporal authority, were central both in the early Caliphate and in the Ottoman Empire and remain important in many places today, like contemporary Saudi Arabia. Such times and places (and this view is, historically and geographically speaking, the norm) should not be understood as monolithically theocratic, as they often are.

Perhaps as a result of this distinction between politically acceptable and more strictly religious ways of life, many Muslim societies historically have been quite tolerant of other faiths (especially "peoples of the book," Christians and Jews and, in India, Hindus), who were of course in error but hardly threats to the established order. Less happily, the separation between religious and governmental authorities, combined with Islam's near monopoly on public legitimacy, may have tended to make authoritative political criticism—and hence the legal or even moral restraint of government—difficult. Political exigency all too often has served as a blanket justification for the actions of Muslim governments. More subtly, Islamic thought has tended to be less institutional than many contemporary Western minds (preoccupied, at least since the French and American Revolutions, with the institutionalization of political aspirations) easily understand.[4]

The Third Understanding: Political Islam

It is necessary to understand the diffidence of traditional Islamic thought toward the institutions of government to have some sense of the radicalism of twentieth-century Islamic political thought. Hasan al-Banna, Abul-Ala Maududi, and others founded organizations (including the Muslim Brotherhood in Egypt and the Jama'at-i Islami in India) and developed a discourse that was simultaneously frankly Islamic and devoted to worldly political goals, and generally conducted outside the ranks of *ulema*. In this view, which Olivier Roy calls "political Islam," the creation of an Islamic state is the very mechanism of salvation, as opposed to the traditional view in which the state is to be endured, although the Islamic virtue of the ruler is desirable. For political Islam, religion is no longer to be thought of as compromised by political life. Instead of tolerance for the status quo, the way people live together—politics in the broadest sense—should be transformed so that Islam is realized here and now. Islam provides a worldview, a vocabulary, a logic, and an ultimate authority for political action. Politics is to be subordinated to the demands of Islam; Islam must leave the confines of the mosque and transform the street, the market, the home, and most of all, the government.

Like Marxism in the nineteenth century, twentieth-century political Islam was a conceptual breakthrough, a new way of thinking, talking about, and so doing politics. Its radicalism was obscured from the West for a number of reasons, including, of course, simple lack of interest, language, distance and other barriers, and the tendency of scholars to combine engagement with objectification that is today criticized under the banner of Orientalism. Less obviously, Western political theory has tended, since the nineteenth century, to be deeply secular, and political Islam is an explicitly theological discourse, even if often conducted by men who are not theologians. Moreover, understanding what was so radical about the emergence of political Islam requires some understanding of what had gone before, in particular, the traditional relationship between *siyasa* and *sharia*, between the ruler and the *ulema*. For whatever reasons, however, the fact remains that a revolutionary discourse was invented and promulgated among millions of people across continents, without drawing substantial intellectual attention from Western policy elites until Khomeini's seizure of power in Iran.

Political Islam provided the conceptual and emotional resources to address desires for modern forms of social and political organization that, in the Arab world and elsewhere, were often couched in the language of Marxism, but without having to disavow God—indeed, with God's authority. Political Islam provided Muslims with an Islamic alternative to the avowedly atheistic grammar of Marxism, so it is perhaps unsurprising that Marxism and political Islam share a great deal. Both discourses can be used to address local issues while simultaneously claiming that local developments are part of a grand progression. And in using a universal discourse to articulate national, even

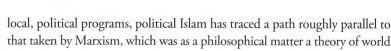

local, political programs, political Islam has traced a path roughly parallel to that taken by Marxism, which was as a philosophical matter a theory of world history but which in practice became the rhetoric of national political movements. Similarly, in practice, political Islam became a language of nationalist politics, but phrased internationally.

The success of political Islam has been considerable. Political Islam became the governing ideology in Afghanistan, Iran, Sudan, and most recently Palestine and arguably Lebanon; became the dominant ideology of protest among Muslims throughout North Africa and the Middle East, in many places threatening the government; and can be heard across Asia. Yet for all its revolutionary significance, Roy maintains that political Islam has failed in some important ways. Islamic revolutions in Afghanistan and Iran have disappointed the victorious revolutionaries. The regime was changed, but politics proceeded too much as before. Islamic revolutions tend to become something else and delegitimize themselves.[5] This is not particularly Islamic; violent efforts to transform society in accordance with transcendent ideals are likely to be disappointing. (Hannah Arendt famously commented that the American Revolution was the only one that went at all well, perhaps because its aims were somewhat modest and its situation, on a rich yet thinly populated continent, was special.[6])

As a system of thought, political Islam has not found a way to address the obdurate mundanity of political life, except by condemnation. Despite contemporary efforts at reform, political Islam currently has little way to articulate the sources, meanings, and significance of government or politics writ large, other than Islam. When political life fails to measure up to the exhortations of Islam, as it must, there is little to be said but to condemn the failings of those involved. (This lesson, too, could have been learned from various instantiations of communism.) Rephrased, political Islam has had great difficulty generating a political discourse that can be meaningfully distinguished from moral discourse. As a result, political Islam is an inadequate language for articulating, or legitimating, institutional life. Politics and institutions still happen, of course, but they do so in ways that cannot be said in authoritative fashion. Much of politics is therefore less than legitimate. Specifically, the dominance of political Islam makes it very difficult to legitimate a modern state—or international law, especially that of human rights—in many places where Western secularism is seen as an unholy imposition, un-Islamic.

Roy's claim that political Islam has failed, however, reflects a specific if widely held understanding of what politics is, namely, the construction and maintenance of a modern state and its impersonal institutions. This is hardly unfair. To establish modern yet Islamic states was, after all, the stated intention of the founders of political Islam. As Roy himself has argued since, however, in a global society, establishing a modern state is not the only and may not be the most important way to understand political life. Indeed, political Islam has spectacularly succeeded in other senses of the word "politics." As mentioned, political Islam remains the dominant discourse in countries inhabited by millions of people. Political Islam has shown its fitness in ideological struggle. While aspects of Marxism and secular Arab nationalism have been incorporated, political Islam has largely supplanted these discourses. Conflicts that were not formerly conceived in Islamist terms now are. Consider the Islamization of the Palestinian struggle, and more recently, the Islamization of much Iraqi and Pakistani politics.

The Fourth Understanding: Neofundamentalism

The failure of political Islam to achieve its modernist aims, namely, the creation of a modern yet Islamic state, hardly represents the end of Islamist politics. In abandoning the narrowly political, in the sense of governmental, understanding of the role of Islam in social life, political Islam has given rise to the quite different politics of neofundamentalism. Just as political Islam addresses the need to operate as a Muslim in the modern world configured by states, neofundamentalism provides a way to be Muslim in a global society.

Like other religions, neofundamentalist Islam has become intensely contemporary by disentangling itself from the matrix of social relations, tradition, and location collectively referred to as "culture" in the old anthropological sense of the set of meanings and folkways that were to be found among a people who lived in a place. Instead, the contemporary believer may adhere to his religion among strangers, in large cities, as an immigrant, precisely because the religion has been pared down to its essentials, a code. The neofundamentalist insistence on the essential requirements of the Koran, which can be practiced most anywhere, serves to make Islam transportable. Islam is where the believer—defined as one who has learned and attempts to follow the code—is. Believers who come together need share very little beyond the code. Hence, neofundamentalist Islamic society is not "culture" in the traditional anthropological sense. Because neofundamentalist Islamic politics comprises believers, there is little need for land, territorial jurisdiction, and most of the rest of the apparatus of the state. Believers may form a community in the flux of great metropolises, even in non-Muslim societies, as throughout Muslim Europe.

Neofundamentalist Islam produces a distinct, and minimalist, understanding of politics, and one diametrically opposed to that of political Islam, precisely on the question of the state. Where political Islam saw the state as the mechanism for the Islamicization of society, in the neofundamentalist view, there is no need to overthrow existing political regimes and establish an Islamic administration. The state can wait. When the worldwide community of believers is sufficiently inclusive, then society, indeed all societies, will be Islamic. The *ummah* then will be in practice as it has always been in principle, universal, and the question of the role of Islam in political life with which this chapter has been concerned will dissolve, as in the days of the Prophet. Until then, a politics that understands itself in terms of a code, easily transportable and transmittable without the institutions of the state, functions quite well in the deterritorialized exchanges of global society.

"Code" here has two meanings. First, the Islamic tradition is, in neofundamentalist circles, stripped down to what is deemed to be its essence. Neofundamentalism is a fundamentalism, and as such, seeks to dispense with ephemera to get at the core of the religion. And what is left is a code, a practice of belief and action. At the same time, and second, a code is a linguistic act, and as such, exemplifies and represents a host of other ways that neofundamentalists and others transmit and so construct "culture."[7] If this were a work of cultural studies (unsurprisingly, there is a growing literature here), we might discuss the following: the "Western" press (with attention to the Danish cartoon imbroglio); the assassination of van Gogh; the successes of al Jazeera; terrorist use of the Internet; bin Laden's intermittent videotapes; the taping of executions, including that of Daniel Berg (a journalist); the assassination of Massoud (by men disguised as journalists); 9/11 as spectacle and the Twin Towers as symbol; the celebrity of bin Laden; the cell phone video of Hussein's hanging; the Abu Ghraib torture pictures; the endless headscarf controversies and now their counterfashions; the broadcasts and e-mail proselytizing of Anwar al-Awaki, who was recently targeted by the not-so-secret CIA—the list could be extended. Such a list of issues (not all of which are, properly speaking, neofundamentalist) suggests a milieu, a vast cultural environment in which accounts are elaborated, sensibilities are constructed, and neofundamentalism emerges as a perspective and even a plausible way of life.

Thus, while its substance may seem archaic to Westerners, neofundamentalist Islam is well suited to the present situation, highly contemporary rather than archaic. In fact, its contemporary character is what is most important about neofundamentalism—it offers a compelling perspective on today's world. To repeat, neofundamentalism offers what for millions of people is an attractive way to see the world now.

Neofundamentalism thus stands in ideological contrast both to the Enlightened vision of modernity traditionally espoused by the United States and (albeit in subtly different ways) its allies and to the perhaps darker conceptions of our future discussed under the rubric of globalization. Centrally important for present purposes, the U.S. National Security Strategy of 2002 was simply wrong in saying (on page 1 no less) that the twentieth century was marked by struggles over ideas but that such struggles are over and that the current wars are with a mysteriously "embittered few," who appear to be disturbingly resilient.[8] In fact, the struggle with radical neofundamentalism is a struggle over how the present time is imagined by many millions.

To summarize, like other ideologies, neofundamentalism has a history and responds to a tradition. Neofundamentalism has developed out of perceptions of the failure of political Islam—itself a revolutionary and relatively recent ideology, developed during the twentieth century—to transform the state and so achieve a truly Islamic society. In contrast to political Islam, neofundamentalism is relatively unconcerned with the institutions of the state and instead seeks to establish community (a new *ummah*) among adherents to a highly codified view of the world. On the basis of this code, neofundamentalists construct a politics of voluntary affiliation (often over the Internet, or in global cities like Hamburg or New York), instead of by mobilizing traditional identities such as tribe, culture, or nation. Neofundamentalism is therefore relatively despatialized, and therefore very well suited to a globalized world. Neofundamentalism is not archaic; it is highly contemporary.

As discussed in Chapter Nine, neofundamentalism can be radicalized by encoding not only a particular kind of religious faith but also a violent understanding of contemporary history, and hence the political and military necessities confronting individual believers. Thus Islamist violence—Global

Jihad—is not a struggle between the modern and the not-yet-modern; it is a struggle over the character of the modern. By being so very contemporary, by providing such a powerful appeal, al-Qaeda forces us to admit that our old stories about what it means to be modern no longer go without saying. In many quarters within very global cities, like London, traditional Western ideas of the modern are increasingly unpersuasive, and the nature of the present is understood otherwise.

CHAPTER EIGHT

ALL POLITICS IS SPATIAL

War and therefore security are increasingly thought of in terms of individuals ("terrorists") and ideologies, rather than nations with land. Rephrased, contemporary conflicts are increasingly understood as contests over social spaces, and only secondarily defined within geographical, physical spaces. The exercise of force and the imposition of the will of the sovereign (quite brutally, the rule of the lawgiver) have come to seem matters of personal, rather than territorial, jurisdiction. This chapter sets itself against these intellectual currents; this chapter argues that to understand military affairs in essentially personal terms is a grave error. All politics is spatial, and that includes military politics.

Military violence has come to seem a matter of people rather than places for a number of reasons, many of them deeply persuasive. If we examine contemporary security threats, we see networks. As discussed in Chapter Seven, terrorists represent no particular place but instead are organized across multiple locations, and many of those places, for example, London or Florida, we regard as friendly. Al-Qaeda was named the base—database—of itinerant jihadists, from many countries, going to fight in many countries. Terrorism is organized over the Internet, a medium with roots in the security policy establishment (ARPANET). Worries about Net-warfare, violence conducted through the Internet, abound. And terrorism is often funded by the sale of illegal drugs, over yet another transnational network, while money and arms flow in parallel channels, like the circulation of blood is paralleled by that of lymph.

Such developments may be generalized easily enough: al-Qaeda represents the kind of warfare endemic to globalization. It is already a cliché to draw connections at the philosophical, if not operational, level between al-Qaeda and various forms of anti-globalization. The point to be stressed here, however, is not some substantive ideological affinity between radical neofundamentalism and globalization, or between radical neofundamentalism and (global) anti-globalization protestors. The point here is far simpler: the United States and al-Qaeda both conduct global violent operations.

One of the meanings of globalization is deterritorialization—space matters less than it used to. The basic idea that technology tends to shrink space is familiar enough. For pertinent example, the United States projects force with bombers that can leave their U.S. bases, drop their bombs pretty much anywhere, and return home without refueling. Such deterritorialization has profound human significance. Ideas of culture, how people who inhabit this place live, their tradition and language and beliefs and the patterns of their lives, cannot be translated directly to the contemporary global city, where people of very different backgrounds come together and often form associations. So terrorism may arise in the heart of contemporary cities, like my ancestral Hamburg, without being particularly expressive of that city. By doing so much to overcome the barriers that physical distance places between people, technology thus facilitates, even demands, a shift from geographical space to social space as ways of organizing human interaction, a shift from places to networks. And as al-Qaeda has conclusively demonstrated, such networks can be dangerous.[1]

In response and understandably, we have seen vast efforts on the part of the U.S. and other governments to unravel terrorist networks. Surveillance, often without warrants and on U.S. citizens, has been deemed necessary to uncover "the terrorists." Internet and phone traffic is monitored in hopes of penetrating terrorist networks. (This rather neatly recalls the Cold War contests between espionage and counterespionage, but this time conducted largely on computer monitors.) The effort to achieve homeland security, however, is not exclusively virtual. Once apprehended, suspected terrorists have been held in undisclosed locations, denied access to legal representation, and tortured (even though this is still not really allowed) or sent to countries where torture is allowed in a process known as "rendition." (One of the mordant joys of the law is the precision with which evasion of the law is treated.) All of this, it has been said, is required to roll up terrorist networks.

It is in light of these developments that we must consider the current vogue for Carl Schmitt, the Nazi legal philosopher.[2] Schmitt famously argued that the essence of the political is the distinction between friend and foe, that is, the distinction between those people we would fight *alongside* and those we would fight *against*—Germans and Jews, perhaps. Or, to update the matter, we (how we are to denominate ourselves is a bit unclear) and the terrorists. Schmitt was a strong and very well-trained mind, and there is much to be said about how and why he was wrong, a discussion this book avoids for the simple reason that I am not writing for academics concerned with a dead fellow academic, even a fashionable one. For present purposes, Schmitt stands for the philosophical proposition that politics is about people who can make war, that is, politics is violent, personal, and organized against an enemy. Such a politics is founded on a demonized other, and so by definition employs a chauvinistic nationalism and tends, if circumstances allow, to simple racism. As a Nazi ideologue, a principled Nazi, as it were, Schmitt stands for this, too.

The potential to mobilize for collective violence is certainly a dramatic understanding of what really counts as political, the essence of politics. Like many tough-minded ideas, Schmitt's effort to found politics on enmity (he devotes far less attention to "friend" than to "enemy") is not nearly as rigorous as he intended or as it initially appears to be. Some ideas are inherently capacious, and attempts to reduce them to some essence—to be rigorous— are likely to destroy their meaning. Consider, in addition to the idea of "politics," conceptions such as "markets," "culture," or "history." It is a nineteenth- and hence twentieth-century intellectual habit, but basically unwise, to use such words as much more than brackets.

Most of politics is not about war at all, and claiming that it is amounts to overdramatic speculation, a kind of essentially juvenile (and macho) grandstanding. I have never been in combat, and how I would fight, were there to be violence here, is unknown. The vast majority of people are in similar situations. In the meantime, however, there is no end to politics. Most of politics is about the mundane, the building of roads, the funding of schools, the promotion and evaluation of leaders, and so forth. The point is important for this book, because the purpose of war—I have been arguing— is to establish just this sort of demobilized, even boring, politics, to build schools and pay for the sanitation system and so forth. "Nation-building" is not just the later stages of military operations; it is not just the justification for violence. Nation-building also signifies the construction of order and the establishment of nonviolent forms of political life in place of war.

I mean "in place" quite spatially, that is, not merely as a synonym for "instead." Tip O'Neil, a Boston pol and former speaker of the U.S. House of Representatives, famously maintained that all politics is local.[3] While that may be a stretch, it is true that all exercises of government power are experienced by people who live someplace. The Greek word *polis*, from which our word "political" is of course derived, means "city," a place with a territorial and social geography. Taken together, we might say that all politics is spatial, and more to the point, that the social order that war—if it can be justified at all—seeks to establish is an inherently spatial concept. To impose order and end the war means that where people had been threatened, they may now go about their lives, in peace.

The idea that politics, and therefore war, should be understood in spatial terms presents serious problems. On the one hand, as this chapter has suggested, there are powerful reasons to understand contemporary (postmodern) warfare in deterritorialized terms, as a matter of networks and the people who operate them as opposed to the familiar terms of the modern nation-state and the U.N. Charter, based on territory. On the other hand, this entire book has argued that war should be understood in terms of the political order it seeks to establish and that political order has an ineluctably spatial aspect.

Let me be clear. I do not argue that war *cannot* be understood on essentially personal grounds. Although rhetorically heavy-handed, it here is sensible to recall that genocide is quite conceivable. But one need not argue from the Nazis. Under contemporary circumstances, warfare is likely to be understood as a contest over people rather than land, as a struggle for what the U.S. military chillingly calls "human terrain." And, Chapter Nine explains, al-Qaeda's politics are defined as a struggle between the true believers and the enemies of Islam. True believers may be found in the United States and in Europe, and the enemies of Islam may be found across Arabia. There are no positions in this war; there are allegiances and enemies.

It might seem that Israel, as a territorially defined state, protected by a giant wall, would exemplify a spatial conception of politics and so of violence, although the "Jewish" in "the Jewish state" may give one pause. But even the appearance of a giant wall may be deceiving. The Israeli military regularly ignores the wall, and national borders generally, in pursuit of people believed to be enemies of Israel. Assassination is basic to Israeli military tactics. Turning to larger operations, by tunneling through walls, ceilings, and floors during the siege of Nablus, the Israelis undermined the spatial logic of the city itself.[4] The purpose of this operation was not to occupy and pacify and reconstruct. The purpose was to disrupt and damage and to kill those others.

Two points seem particularly salient for Americans. First, Israeli violence is almost inevitably explained in defensive terms. Perhaps assassination, pardon, targeted killing, is a form of self-defense, but little else could be said. To argue that such killing is an exercise of power, and should be evaluated on political terms—to make the kind of argument that this book has tried to make—would commit the Israelis to being responsible for the areas in which they wage war, that is, would commit the Israelis to further and deeper occupation, which as a matter of domestic politics appears to be impossible. And so Israel assumes a defensive, if not entirely plausible, posture. Second, strategically and constitutionally, I leave the reader with the question of whether Israeli foreign policy, including military policy, over the last generation or so should be judged a success.

If we look at the United States, we see a similar shift from territorial to personal organization of violence, from taking hills to body bags as the metric of military success. This is not entirely new. We have always counted our own casualties, and in Vietnam, the United States began measuring its performance in terms of enemy people killed (once they are dead, we must call them enemies if we possibly can).[5] But the personalization (deterritorialization) of warfare has come a long way since the Vietnam War. The "Global War on Terror" spawned an enormous apparatus for the detection, apprehension, interrogation, detention, and eventual punishment of terrorists. Territorial jurisdiction, an understanding of where, geographically, power may be exercised, is mocked by the practice of rendition, in which the CIA flies individuals to distant and legally convenient places. The "Global War on Terror" (like the Israeli raids and bin Laden's War) was essentially a war on people denominated enemies, rather than a struggle for the control of land and the establishment of order someplace. In fact, we now wage war using drones in countries with which we are nominally at peace. More generally, we now tend to understand security concerns in social, even personal, terms, in lieu of the territory that traditionally defined the nation-state and its wars.

The shift from understanding security geographically to understanding security socially makes it difficult for us to think politically about our warfare. Bluntly, if the goal of security policy is to kill the terrorists (and surely killing the enemy is a common enough goal in warfare), then we may blind ourselves to questions of how those we do not kill, the survivors, are to make a new society. Space is necessarily a part of politics—again, the *polis* is a city, a milieu—and in focusing on those we consider the enemy (or, from the other side, an obsession with the infidel Americans), we lose sight of the ultimately more important question: how do we create a workable, perhaps even good, social order?

Barring another terrorist attack on the scale of 9/11, however, it will be claimed that, for all its costs, our security apparatus is a success. But we should not forget the costs. "Human terrain" suggests not only the use of academic anthropology for military ends but a range of ways in which the control of bodies, rather than the control of places, is the objective of our collective violence. Consider the range stretching from wiretapping, to surveillance, to the destruction of personal autonomy, to the denial of *habeas corpus*, to rendition, to torture, to assassination (i.e., targeted killing, surely better than indiscriminate killing, no?), to secret bombings—is our policy worthy? Is this how we wish to fight?

And is such fighting successful? The nation has lost more people in Iraq than it did on 9/11. This factoid might be irrelevant if one thinks Iraq has nothing to do with terrorism, as is sometimes claimed. But even if Iraq and terrorism were separate when the last round of fighting began, they are no longer separable issues—it's all very confused, which is hardly a sign of a coherent foreign or military policy. Both Iraq and Afghanistan are giving every appearance of being very long wars indeed. But our lack of success should hardly be surprising. We appear to have forgotten what politics is about, including the importance of place. To the extent that we do not understand what politics is, our military efforts to establish political order are rudderless.

"Human terrain" might also be understood to signal something more promising than understanding the enemy as object and justification, bringing us a long way down the road Schmitt mapped. Human terrain is evil imagery, but the phrase reminds us that war is about humans, and the social spaces they create among themselves. Perhaps such tough-minded inaccuracy is required to wean many people in the security community from their tendency to rely on weapons, the simplicity of violence, and thereby to avoid political labors, their real jobs.

This is a new and different world, and we are confronted with questions of political form. As a theoretical matter, it is tempting to say that the quintessential modern political form, the nation-state, is ill-suited to cope with the postmodern conditions created by globalization, which has its violence in the form of radical neofundamentalism, even when the nation in question is as protean as the United States. As a political matter, it is tempting to say that nations, like Israel and now the United States, must evolve in order to survive in the new environment. One must establish networks in order to fight networks. In a despatialized world, warfare must become despatialized, too.

The characteristic temptation presented by grand history ("this time is really important") is to draw excessive (hubristic?) normative conclusions. The rise of the nation-state did not make the medieval city obsolete, though it did shift the grounds of political life. Similarly, globalization cannot do without the nation-state in various ways. In particular, and as discussed below, a nation, the United States, finds itself concerned with constructing and maintaining a global security order. Rephrased, the society emerging from those processes we call globalization, the City of Gold, is hardly complete (in that sense, perfect), or sufficient. Similarly, while neofundamentalism is a new form of political life, and this is a new war, the mere fact of historical emergence hardly requires us to concede the historical ground to our enemies. Bluntly put, we do not have to become our enemies in order to defeat them.

But how is the United States, functioning as a nation, to project force, in a global context? Thus stated as a matter of abstract theory, this problem may appear more daunting than it, in fact, is. Thinking through those processes we somewhat vaguely indicate with "globalization" is vitally important to understanding the way we live and fight, now. But such thinking can easily be overdone. Change is never total; globalization is not everything.

Suppose we acknowledge that deterritorialization is a useful concept; our relationship to geographical space is changing; and technology is a big part of the reason why. What does this mean for warfare? Does it mean that militaries are replaced by networks, and the paradigm of combat is assassination? I do not think so.

Even in the heyday of nationalism, political thought was never about geography as such. To think politically about a nation is to think about a social space mapped onto a corresponding geographical space. For many purposes, however, including many military purposes, the social/political could be understood in geographical terms, and vice versa. "France" and "the French" are tightly corresponding terms. Traditionally, conquest of the one entailed conquest of the other. When "the Union" (explicitly a political order) conquered "the South" (explicitly a region, which declared itself a nation), the Civil War was over. This has changed. When the United States conquered Afghanistan, or Iraq, the war had only just begun. Thus social and geographical spaces have, for military purposes important to the United States, become decoupled.

But the fact that "Iraq" and "Iraqi" are not, for some military and other purposes, tightly corresponding terms does not mean that Iraq, the place, does not need peace. Moreover, "Iraq" is also a symbol, like "Palestine," which plays a role in the global milieu in which contemporary politics is done. Therefore, management of a place (on the relatively local, tactical, operational, and theater level) becomes, at the same time, symbolically significant globally, politically, and so strategically. Geography thus reasserts itself. By the same token, the people of the United States and indeed the world are unusually aware of Afghanistan. From this perspective, our politics has not been decoupled from geography at all. Perhaps, one might well say, this "Afghanistan" is only an image or a simulacrum, not "the real" Afghanistan—which is to say that political life lacks a certain veracity—surely not a new insight.

Rediscovering the classics should remind us that, to the extent possible, we should not let the sometimes dazzling fact of historical change blind us to historical continuity. Those processes discussed under the rubric of globalization, and the rise of new forms of politics, including terrorist networks, mean at the very least that we must think carefully. Such developments do not mean that the human condition has become altogether different, that old wisdom is suddenly useless. Networks, too, constitute social spaces, and stripped of their geographical associations, many of the old rules still apply. By way of example and analogy, the fact that securities exchanges are computerized networks, rather than physical meeting places, does not mean that ancient concerns about membership, payment, settlement, dispute adjudication, and fraud no longer matter. So, to return to the concern with which this chapter opened, the United States indeed must recognize that this is a new kind of war. At the same time, even as we operate in this brave new deterritorialized world, the nation finds itself committed to a very old-fashioned project, the establishment of political order, safe spaces for human fruition, in lieu of chaos.

This Part Two has argued that

1. U.S. security policy should be rethought as global political engagement to win at least tacit support for a global security order. Bureaucratic redescription of threats, combined with contingency planning, is insufficient (Chapter Four).
2. Political engagement requires us to understand noncitizens, and even those who might be our adversaries, as political subjects (Chapter Five).
3. Political engagement requires us to understand ourselves to be living at the same time in history as our contemporaries, rather than being somehow ahead of them. Modernity is shared (Chapter Six).
4. Conversely, political engagement requires us to understand others, especially our adversaries, to be, like us, attempting to construct the future. It is precisely their vision of the future that we contest (Chapter Seven).
5. A security order, and politics more generally, are fundamentally spatial, as opposed to personal, concepts (Chapter Eight).

PART THREE

THE CHALLENGE
OF RADICAL
NEOFUNDAMENTALISM

CHAPTER NINE

BIN LADEN'S CHALLENGE

Consider the possibility that, for bin Laden, violence is not an instrument of policy, a way for the state to achieve its interests. Al-Qaeda has no worldly interests prior to its violence; al-Qaeda is constituted through and for the sake of violence directed against those it tautologically declares to be enemies of the *ummah*. Violence itself is the soul of al-Qaeda's politics. If this is true, then bin Laden has created a new form of political organization, and in consequence, a new kind of warfare, and therefore, a new kind of threat, to which our security policy must respond.

This may seem to give our enemy too much credit. But our antagonism to the man should not blind us to the fact that bin Laden, like Marx, is both a key participant in and a symbol of historical developments. Bin Laden has militarized neofundamentalism, creating a new form of political association I call radical neofundamentalism. Obviously, Islamist violence, and particularly radical neofundamentalism, present serious tactical, operational, and strategic challenges to the security and diplomatic communities. But more deeply still, the militarization of neofundamentalism fundamentally changes the security environment in which the United States operates. Bin Laden thus requires the United States to rethink force projection more generally, the enterprise of this Part Three. Bin Laden is, in short, important enough to force us to adapt, just as the emergence of the Soviet Union forced us to adapt, however we might have wished to dismiss communism as an intellectual matter.

The republican and existential challenge, of course, is to respond to this threat without losing sight of who we are.

To rethink force projection in a security environment transformed by the emergence of al-Qaeda, we need to have a deeper sense of what it means to say that bin Laden and others have radicalized neofundamentalist politics. Rephrased, we need to specify the political logic that informs, and that is expressed by, al-Qaeda's violence. This logic, which runs through a great deal of radical discourse, may be synthetically articulated thus:[1]

> The failure to establish a global *ummah* is not due to the limitations of political Islam as a discourse or for some other internal reason. Instead, the establishment of the global *ummah* has been blocked by unbelievers, that is, by those outside the *ummah* (and hence in the *dar ul-harb*, the domain of war). In fact, the *ummah* is under constant attack, sometimes overtly (as in Afghanistan, Bosnia, Chechnya, and Iraq) and often covertly, through the oppression of Muslim countries and discrimination against Muslims living in non-Muslim lands. If one needed to be convinced of this apocalyptic vision, evidence can be found easily enough. Most importantly, because Islam is the truth, what—besides a massive conspiracy—could prevent the flourishing of the *ummah*? And what further evidence of such conspiracy does one need besides the unwavering American support for Israel's brutal domination of Palestine and its other neighbors? Or the West's unquenchable thirst for Muslim oil? Or the ghettoization of and discrimination against Muslims in many Western societies? Even many non-Muslims in the West admit such things. The time for a truly Islamic politics has not yet arrived. The struggle against the enemies of Islam is the sufficient—indeed the only practical—step *toward* achieving a truly Islamic society. For now, Islamic politics is about organizing for struggle and executing operations.[1]

We arrive at our political positions, that is, political stances must always also be understood, diachronically. Indeed, Thomas Friedman has very publicly argued that the radical neofundamentalism of Nidal Malik Hasan (Forth Hood) rests on what he simply calls "The Narrative":

> the cocktail of half-truths, propaganda and outright lies about America that have taken hold in the Arab-Muslim world since 9/11. Propagated by ji-

hadist Web sites, mosque preachers, Arab intellectuals, satellite news stations and books—and tacitly endorsed by some Arab regimes—this narrative posits that America has declared war on Islam, as part of a grand "American-Crusader-Zionist conspiracy" to keep Muslims down.[2]

The similarity of the position sketched here not just to Marxism, but even more to anarchism in its revolutionary mode, is unmistakable: actual, institutional politics is deferred and becomes utopian (both very good and very vague). In place of institutional politics there is struggle, ideological and sometimes violent, and the limited organization required by the supporters of the struggle.[3] It is true that the establishment of the Caliphate is often said to be the purpose of Global Jihad. But the Caliphate is a rhetorical gesture, a horizon for violent action, not a political program in the ordinary sense. Global Jihad is waged mostly in non-Muslim lands or on the borders of the Muslim world. Those who wage Global Jihad have made no efforts to name a caliph, to persuade the Muslim world of his authority, or to raise him to power in some Muslim land. "The Caliphate" is a placeholder, the place to which the world will be brought when enough violence has done enough work.[4]

Global Jihad expresses a political logic of great purity. If the forces arrayed against the *ummah* prevent its flourishing, then *anything*—including the immolation of one's own children—that can be done to hurt those forces is a victory. Political Islam's violent aspirations for truly Islamic states, associated with the radical Sayyid Qutb, may be postponed in favor of radical neo-fundamentalism's (bin Laden's) aspirations for violence per se.[5] Politics need not be about creating institutions through which large numbers of people live among one another and societies function. Instead, politics can be nothing more than the organization that makes the waging of Global Jihad possible.

The attacks of September 11 spectacularly demonstrated that mere violence, mass death, is relatively easy to achieve. No durable institutions are necessary. It suffices to organize just enough people to cause harm, no more. Bin Laden has made violence constitutive of a network (al-Qaeda), a loose polity, without significantly encumbering the polity by locating it geographically or giving it a burdensome institutional structure. Like neo-fundamentalism more generally, al-Qaeda is so unencumbered that it may be better considered "virtual," as an ideology—a code—that can be replicated by small groups of people, or even individuals, at any time or place the conditions allow. September 11 may somewhat disconcertingly, but not inaccurately, be thought of as war by an NGO (nongovernmental organization). As a corollary, and as discussed in Chapter One, bin Laden has made it somewhat picayune to insist on discussing war exclusively in terms of the state.

Like viruses, terrorist groups may be small, easily replicated, capable of doing great damage, and hard to destroy. This viral militarism is new, and—along with its roots in the relatively new form of neofundamentalism—is a large part of why bin Laden represents a rupture with Muslim tradition. Historically, jihad (in its specific meaning of war, rather than the word's broader and deeper sense of struggle, including spiritual and armed struggles) was waged in societies, for example, the Ottoman Empire, with armies, territories, folk, and the like. As a practical matter, social institutions served as constraints. From the perspective of Global Jihad, however, institutions (a marketplace, a university, even a mosque, and even in a Muslim country like Pakistan) are merely targets, part of the irredeemable contemporary order.

As a doctrinal matter, bin Laden's radical step was to declare that every individual had the right, indeed the obligation, to declare and wage war against the enemies of the *ummah*. Consonantly, many radicals have claimed that they (not the *ulema*) had the right to *takfir*, that is, the right to declare a fellow Muslim to be impious (*kafir*), and hence apostate, for which the penalty was usually execution or expulsion. For many, war, which had been a collective and political act, was thereby radically decentralized, even individualized. In principle, anyone can organize a jihadist group to fight against the *ummah's* true enemies (however defined and often Muslim), and many such groups have been established, jihad *à la carte*. And so bin Laden's forces became viral; Global Jihad became a way of being.[6]

At this point, we can begin to see how badly our habitual understandings of warfare account for violence conceived as Global Jihad. Traditionally, security is understood in terms of states with various interests, interests that may be in conflict. If the conflict is sufficiently severe and is not otherwise resolved, the conflict may be decided militarily. From bin Laden's perspective, fighting against the United States in Iraq (regardless of the cost to an Iraqi future?) or bombing in London are justified, but not because such actions are expected to inspire a specific change in U.S. or British policy. Nor can such actions be thought of as an effort by al-Qaeda to achieve its own political goals; al-Qaeda has almost no political interests to express. The members of the Hamburg cell who participated in 9/11 left Germany for training in Afghanistan with the intention of waging jihad in Chechnya. They were redirected to United States.[7] Violence against the enemies of the *ummah* is its own reward. Which enemies, and what results the violence is intended to bring about, do not matter very much. This is not Clausewitz's "policy by other means," for the simple reason that the policy has no substance independent of the violence. The essential political interest of radicalized neofundamentalism is the conflict itself. Al-Qaeda thus presents—at least conceptually, ideologically—a strikingly pure enemy, not because "they hate us for our freedom," but because their war is encoded in their political organization.

Western minds (including my own) tend to rebel at the effort to think of violence "merely" as a step toward a future *ummah*, which seems perilously close to pure nihilism or what has rather floridly been called a "cult of death."[8] After all, violence, we reason, must have a reason, must be a means to some end. And has not bin Laden made various political demands (regarding Saudi Arabia, and then Israel, and then Iraq) and even a few gestures (perhaps empty) toward negotiation, at least with Europeans? Not really. If we look at al-Qaeda, actual politics—beyond operational organization and propaganda—is hard to find. Bin Laden has not attempted to take over a state, not even Afghanistan. He has shown little interest in institutions apart from those necessary to his war. Nor has bin Laden shown any sustained interest in other issues of concern to Muslims, such as health care, education, or economic development. Even warfare, the idea of "making jihad" is unfocused, evidently because the purpose is struggle against the enemies of the *ummah,* not the achievement of specific results. Al-Qaeda has made no real efforts to negotiate, in contrast, for example, with the PLO. Indeed, much antiterrorism policy, for example, regarding captured airplanes, traditionally assumed that the act of violence was a move in a negotiation. But suicide bombing does not work that way.[9] In short, it is difficult to discern any evidence of real politics in al-Qaeda, or in recent attacks in Texas, Michigan, or New York.[10]

On reflection, however, perhaps the lack of political content in Global Jihad should not be so surprising. Indeed, what ordinary political goods could a neofundamentalist group want? Neofundamentalism constitutes itself through the creation of associations, groups of people who share codes, not institutions. The near nihilism of al-Qaeda is merely the violent expression of the political minimalism that defines neofundamentalism. The fact that bin Laden and other terrorists offer political-sounding explanations for their actions hardly constitutes doing politics. Just because members of the Baader-Meinhof Gang spouted bad Marxism, or Timothy McVeigh talked in terms of the Constitution, does not mean that such terrorism should be understood in terms of its rhetoric, that the Red Army Faction was about achieving communism or McVeigh could be explained by the twists and turns of constitutional thought or history.[11] The widely heard proposition to the effect that al-Qaeda's terrorism must be explicable by some ordinary political rationale, that is, that the explicit ideology of Global Jihad may be safely ignored, seems to be due mostly to habit and is an example of mirroring, the thoughtless assumption that others see the world as we do. There is nothing in the nature of collective violence that *requires* warfare to be the conduct of politics, understood in an Enlightened sense, with the addition of other means.[12] Clausewitz was a strategist, a teacher, a theorist of modernity, and, like all Germans of his age, deeply influenced by Kant—he was writing of the logic of the ideals encoded within his society, including a protomodern state, confronting a populist enemy (the Grand Armee), with the aid of a professional military (the General Staff).

Contra the ordinary (superficial) reading of Clausewitz, war on the ground can be many things. The relationship of social organization to violence within radical neofundamentalism, the way violence is encoded, is different from the scripting of violence in a bureaucratic nation-state, or in the cadres of a separatist movement, or even in political Islam, which endeavors to seize control of the mechanisms of the state, thereby acquiring responsibility, entanglement. Such responsibilities would inevitably conflict with the duty to wage Global Jihad, would in effect undercut the authority of the code by making worldly demands, by requiring ordinary politics rather than ceaseless struggle against "the enemy." Since violence is not an instrument of policy, a way for the state to achieve objectives decided upon elsewhere, bin Laden has reversed Clausewitz, and thereby switched the polarity of security thinking. For bin Laden, violence is not a means to a politically determined end. Violence is an end in itself. In creating a new form of politics devoted to this proposition, bin Laden has invented a new kind of threat to the United States.

This threat to the United States is a structural part of radical neofundamentalism.[13] Ideologically, it hardly matters that the United States does not see itself, and does not want to be seen, as the far enemy or, as Ayatollah

Khomeini put it, the Great Satan. It does not matter if the United States claims it is not the enemy of Islam. Once politics is understood to be the production of violence, then conversely, violence is politically required, and the identification of a threat can be expected. Bin Laden needs his enemies—we are the enemy because we occupy that position in the structure of radical neofundamentalism. And if our status as the enemy is required by the logic of Global Jihad, then we may be assured that we will be portrayed as the enemy, over and over again, regardless of our actions; that suicides and other losses will be replenished through recruitment; that new volunteers will be encouraged. And sufficiently angered and in the nature of war, we will commit actions that are reprehensible to us and others and for which we will be blamed. Liberties will be trampled. Sensibilities abused. We will assassinate, sometimes in error. Mistakes will be made. Innocent lives will be lost.

Even without misdeeds on our part, however, it is not too difficult to cast us as the enemy. Quite apart from the two ongoing wars in Muslim countries, without universal conversion, and the thoroughgoing reform of most of the people who understand themselves to be Muslims, the *ummah*, the community of true believers, may always be portrayed as under siege. From within the logic of Global Jihad, every action that threatens the *ummah* increases the demand for and the allure of terrorism. In particular, the more successful the United States is perceived to be, the more fighting the United States seems to constitute a sufficient "Islamic" politics.

What could be a more perfect expression of a politics of negation than suicide bombing, Global Jihad's most riveting technique? Although developed as a tactic by Sri Lanka's Tamil Tigers, who long fought what appears to be a conceptually rather conventional war of separatist liberation, suicide bombing as used by al-Qaeda is a horrifyingly concise expression of this new antipolitics. If the purpose of political life is violence, then once violence has been achieved, political life, life among other people, can be reckoned complete, and hence finished—in the same instant, in fact.

Jihad has always been understood primarily as a spiritual struggle, even when it involved physical violence. (It was widely reported that the 9/11 bombers believed they could enjoy sins like lap dancing and booze because all would be forgiven once they had succeeded in killing so many people.) Rituals of isolating the bomber-to-be, of wrapping him in white, and of promises (usually kept) of elaborate funerals and photographs postmortem help the bomber to understand himself (somehow more horrifyingly, some-times herself), as already gone, an inhabitant more of the next world than of this. Suicide bombing is thus—like some forms of monasticism—an effort to be otherworldly. But this "otherworldliness" should not be overdone. Suicide bombing is not only self-destruction but also killing. The suicide bomber tries to create as much pain in this world as possible, that is, bombing is intended to affect others and is, in that minimal sense, political. Moreover, and practi-cally speaking, the next world is reached through elaborate planning and or-ganization in this world, that is, suicide bombing missions require some degree of organization. This is politics, if *de minimis*, at the vanishing point.

To dwell on the horrible and obvious, suicide bombing is not fruitful, a point made more awful when one considers how young many bombers are. A bombing operation limits itself in time and in scope. Sooner or later, the plan is executed or perhaps abandoned or foiled. The attack may be carried out or not but, at any rate, is over. More generally, while political Islam rests on intense, even millenarian, hopes for politics (the Islamicization of society through the establishment of Islamic states), radical neofundamentalism de-spairs of political life in a global context. Through undertaking Global Ji-had, the political wills of radical neofundamentalists are devoted to death, and hence the negation of lives that might have built a better society.

One may be forgiven the brutal thought that a political ideology and actual movement that is most perfectly expressed by suicide cannot last very long. Less brutally, not so long ago, it was widely thought that the contemporary wave of terrorism was carried out by individuals who shared specific formative experiences and that once those men were killed, neutralized, or simply grew old, then the security threat would pass. And indeed anarchism, after killing U.S. presidents and precipitating World War I, rather suddenly ceased to be a historical force. But after 9/11, many terrorists were killed, in al-Qaeda, the Taliban, and other Islamist groups, and the organizations continue to thrive, because they continue to be able to recruit new adherents. Instead of being dismissed as an ephemeral phenomenon, this book has argued that radical neofundamentalism should be understood as articulating a sadly persuasive narrative in which the United States plays the role famously given us by the Ayatollah Khomeini, the Great Satan, the enemy of the *ummah*. We must, of course, seek to subvert this logic. But we are at some level and to some extent literally compelled by violence. Violent actions form their own bonds and commitments; we are fighting because we have been fighting and have debts to collect. And so we fight Muslims, and must therefore be enemies of the *ummah*, no? Violence still begets violence.

There is no policy step that can be taken that will transform the role, *within bin Laden's play*, of the United States into something other than the crusader nation. While Muslims, including radical neofundamentalists, may in fact be angry over the actions of the U.S. government, it is foolish to believe that terrorist violence is some sort of logical response to U.S. government policy and that changes in U.S. politics will convince terrorists to abjure violence. Terrorist violence is a response to perceived evil, who we are ("crusaders," or better, "devils"), not what we have done, as horrible as that may be (what else is to be expected from a devil?).

The question, then, is how to fight. May we hope for more than the ruthlessness implicit in understanding this war as an unavoidable clash of civilizations, between a Western version of bureaucratic modernity and the enthusiastic nihilism of Global Jihad, in which the two sides have no language with which to talk to one another, no way to negotiate a peace? I believe the answer to be yes. Global Jihad must not only be combated by force of arms but be *supplanted* by different politics, in which violence in support of an idealized *ummah* is not sufficient for political life. Rephrased, Global Jihad will be over when vanishingly few Muslims believe that the *ummah* can be constituted by suicide, when few of any creed believe that politics is no more than killing. The rest of this book will consider what we may do to speed that day.

So, just how many people may be fairly described as radical neofundamentalists? Military thinkers, in particular, want to know how substantial the threat is. In Pakistan, I was often told that the vast majority of people are peace loving, that perhaps "1 percent" of the population are "terrorists." Although that estimate may be high, in a country that will soon count 180 million souls, 1 percent of the population is some 1,800,000 people. No doubt the percentage in the United States is much lower, but suppose, *arguendo*, that 0.1 percent of the population, 1 in 1,000, may be inclined to terrorist acts—that is still some 300,000 people. Three hundred thousand barely organized people is not enough, of course, to conquer and rule Pakistan, the United States, or most places, nor does it pose a threat to the military as such. But, as discussed above, if the purpose of violence is merely to hurt people, rather than to establish dominion, then few warriors are required. Individuals and small groups can do a great deal of damage, as demonstrated regularly. Understandably enough, societies have taken measures designed to thwart such low-probability yet very harmful attacks. Security measures have substantially degraded the way we live in the United States and Europe and have nearly paralyzed countries like Pakistan. So, objectively, I think it is fair to say that radical neofundamentalism, "The Narrative," poses a profound security threat.

That said, putatively objective risk analysis poses its own problems. *This chapter describes certain conceptual positions*, which is not quite the same thing as a psychological stance or even a political position. In the process of explanation, such positions tend to be rendered with greater clarity than they have in real life. This is unsurprising and to some degree unavoidable. At the same time, ideas—ideals, symbols—really do matter. If I were to discuss more familiar ideas that Americans care a great deal about, such as "democracy" or "freedom" or "the rule of law," my text would be contestable, partial, certainly simplified. But the fact that any specific expression of such ideas, on which my discussion would have to rely, would slight other important matters does not somehow imply that "democracy," for example, is unimportant to Americans, or not worth fighting for, however difficult it may be to find an agreed-upon articulation. Precisely because concepts like "democracy" or "jihad" mean many things at once, and life lived under the banner of such concepts means many things more, and texts must compromise, we must be careful to understand the difference between a text offered as explanation, what Weber called a heuristic device, and the social reality that the text seeks to clarify in some way.

The extent to which "Global Jihad" accurately explains contemporary Islamist violence is difficult to assess empirically and will remain so. "Why do people fight?" is rarely a simple question. Ideologies tend to be mixed and sloppy. People change ideas, hold mutually conflicting ideas at the same time, and often simply have not thought very deeply, or do not even know what they think. So the description of radical neofundamentalism and therefore Global Jihad presented here is rather stylized, too clear, and overly logical to be a very accurate description of social or psychological reality.

This book is not sociology or cultural studies. Instead, I am trying to consider what our conflict with Islamist violence, including our wars in Afghanistan and Iraq, might mean for U.S. security policy, and more deeply, for our understanding of ourselves as a nation. This book is not offered as a description of the wars themselves, nor a guide to their prosecution. It must be emphasized, in particular, that factions—and so violence—can be organized in many ways, and are. Within Islam, and quite apart from the ideological schema laid out in this chapter, there are divisions, of which Sunni and Shi'ite are only the most famous. Nationalisms, even of relatively "artificial" nations, such as Iraq, matter. So do tribes, many of which span national borders. Afghanistan in particular is famous for loyalties to clan, village, and valley, even within tribes—tribes inside of tribes. Economics (including smuggling, banditry, looting and other illegitimate behavior) matters. And so forth.

But while Global Jihad does not explain the war(s), it needs to be understood. As a security matter, the empirical question of how important bin Laden's ideology (or any ideology, including our own) is to this or that group of fighters is not only unanswerable (perennially available as a subject for future dissertations) but moot. Global Jihad is clearly important. It is a narrative through which a great deal of violence, including September 11 and more recent attacks on the United States, has been organized and, as such, represents a substantial threat—and how we respond to such threats also matters.

The understanding—the narrative—of what it means to be waging Global Jihad appears to be an evolving one. As presented above, radical neo-fundamentalism differed from political Islam on the question of the state, in either/or fashion. In France, where Islamist control of the state is inconceivable, or Algeria, where controlling the state was everything, such a dichotomy makes considerable sense, at least for analytic purposes. But in the early stages of insurgency, in say Pakistan, when political responsibility is not an immediate concern, the two ideologies may be quite complementary. So the Taliban appears to desire to reassert control over the mechanisms of the state in Afghanistan and quite possibly Pakistan. At the same time, such "national" efforts may also be understood in the context of Global Jihad. From this perspective, the distinction between the Taliban and al-Qaeda is not particularly important, and the destruction of al-Qaeda's operational capability may mean, as an ideological matter, very little. Al-Qaeda "doesn't need much organization anymore—just push out The Narrative over the Web and satellite TV, let it heat up humiliated, frustrated, or socially alienated Muslim males, and one or two will open fire on their own. See: Major Hasan."[14]

To close this chapter on a more optimistic note: the slippage between our world and our conceptions of it offers opportunities. Vagaries and inconsistencies make careful thought difficult but, more importantly for present purposes, give us opportunities to do politics. Precisely because our ideas are incomplete and inconsistent, even when confronted with enemies, we may appeal to better natures, to other commitments. Within the logic of Global Jihad, we are the enemy and no politics is possible. But I strongly doubt there are many people who live entirely within any single logic, including that of Global Jihad. Within the real worlds that each of us actually inhabits, there are many logics, and the question is how to find ways of making peaceful politics, a *modus vivendi*, possible.

CHAPTER TEN

IDEOLOGICAL ABSTRACTION
AND CONCRETE PRESENCE

The ideological character of Global Jihad makes it difficult to contest. It is hard even to think about Global Jihad in any deep way, not only because radical neofundamentalism is a profoundly different worldview that Americans generally abhor but also because it is difficult to take the belief system of an enemy entirely seriously. They are, after all, the enemy, and understanding for the enemy is close to sympathy and so psychologically difficult, even if militarily desirable. And Americans pride themselves on being a practical folk, so we may find it difficult to think about these very real wars—what could be more concrete?—as conflicts with another worldview. More practically still, important forces within the U.S. security community are likely to resist understanding their wars as admittedly abstract conflicts with a postmodern ideology of political negation. Who has time for such intellectualism?

There are many ways to avoid thought. Bureaucracies often avoid thinking about the beliefs of others by what analysts call mirror imaging, rather unself-consciously assuming that other people think in their terms. Americans see themselves as pragmatists, and so other people must be similarly averse to ideology, right? And U.S. military policy has often been driven by an inappropriate expectation of "rationality" on the part of the enemy, that is, by the assumption that the enemy will think like members of the U.S. security community and act accordingly. The wars in both Vietnam and

Iraq have rather conclusively demonstrated that people will fight even when it is demonstrably irrational to do so, at least as people like Secretaries of Defense Robert McNamara and Donald Rumsfeld appear to have understood "rational." To make matters worse, in efforts to shift the cost-benefit analyses of its enemies (to make "the rational" more obvious), the U.S. military has found itself escalating conflicts, doing collateral damage that hardly lessened hostilities and that was strategically counterproductive.

When we (military and civilians alike) do consider enemy ideology, we tend to understand it not on its own terms but as a means to conceptualize who the enemy is, thereby producing the symmetry required for warfare. So we speak of "the terrorists" as once we spoke of "the communists." This identification of people (enemies, who may be targeted, "the bad guys") by their ideas may be tactically necessary but, at the same time, represents a fundamental shift of attention from the substance of ideas to labels to the people so labeled, perhaps as bad guys. This is convenient. If people are the problem, then we can solve the problem by addressing the people, often by undertaking military operations against them. The abstract ideological problem is thus considered, but only to be immediately replaced by a far more concrete, even tactical, problem. So we rather easily convince ourselves that we do not need to think about radical neofundamentalism—we just need to know who is a terrorist, so we can send a drone.

While intelligence and military efforts to prevent terrorism, and to combat identified terrorists, will and should continue, one should not be too hopeful here. Specific people, enemy fighters, are not the only or even the most important problem. Ideas, too, can be dangerous, and very hard to fight. *An idea cannot be killed.* As a corollary, this war cannot be "won" in the conventional sense. Seizing territory or even taking capitals may be necessary but are ancillary activities. Killing terrorists may be required, but we cannot "kill the terrorists" and win the war, as President Bush suggested, because "the terrorists" are not a stable population of people who can be identified and then subdued.[1] Instead, the terrorists are those who at some point adopt, and act on, an ideology such as bin Laden's. As a Jordanian intelligence officer quoted in *The Atlantic* put it, bin Laden "created the concept of al-Qaeda and all of its offshoots. He feels he's achieved his goal. . . . Osama bin Laden is like Karl Marx. Both created an ideology. Marxism still flourished well after Marx's death. And whether bin Laden is killed, or simply dies of natural causes, al-Qaedism will survive him."[2] Inversely, it is difficult to imagine how, within our current conceptual framework, we can wean ourselves from killing perceived enemies of the state in the nether regions of the planet.

So long as radical neofundamentalism remains a convincing worldview, Global Jihad will be a threat. And, to make matters worse and as already suggested, from within the logic of Global Jihad, every action that threatens the *ummah* strengthens the logic and increases the allure of terrorism. In particular, the more successful the United States is perceived to be, the more that fighting the United States seems to constitute a sufficiently "Islamic" politics, the more we may expect somebody like Faisal Shahzad to plant a bomb someplace like Times Square. Thus locally successful military action may actually worsen the security situation, an idea familiar as the notion that the more terrorists we kill, the more we create. To shift metaphors, in our engagements in Afghanistan, Iraq, and elsewhere, we may be struggling to dig ourselves out of a hole.

Such thinking suggests a rather traditional isolationism, but isolating this conflict is not a real possibility. Even in the unlikely event that the United States (and all other societies?) were suddenly to abandon oil in favor of other sources of energy, even were the United States to cease supporting Israel, global security and humanitarian concerns preclude allowing the Middle East to operate outside the security order. Not that the problem is limited to the Middle East: Global Jihad is, as the name suggests, global, deterritorialized to an extent never seen before. Despite all the talk about Muslim lands, there is no frontier in this war. It is therefore futile to hope that radical neofundamentalism can be geographically contained.

Radical neofundamentalism cannot be defeated directly, because ideas cannot be destroyed, but they can be replaced. As did the Cold War, this war will end when minds change. Therefore, *the strategic objective of the United States is to see that radical neofundamentalism is supplanted by other ideologies.* Radical fundamentalism must be rendered literally passé, over, a bad dream.

The political imaginations that will make radical neofundamentalism, and hence Global Jihad, old-fashioned must be responsive to Muslim sensibilities. As discussed in Chapter Five, the idea that politics tends to become more secular with the passage of time is a myth of the Enlightenment, not borne out by history in the Islamic world, nor, for that matter, in the United States. Political Islam has been such a success because it gave voice to many of the concerns of the revolutionary left, but in a Muslim idiom— Marx without the atheism. And if one can have God and politics, then why settle for mere politics? Across the Middle East, perhaps most obviously in Palestine, "secular" political movements and parties have been displaced by their "Islamic" counterparts. There is no reason to believe that the political imaginations that supplant bin Laden's in the minds of Muslims will not be similarly expressed in terms of Islam and responsive to the concerns of Muslims as Muslims.

The Islamic political imaginations that supplant radical neofundamentalism also must be as contemporary as radical fundamentalism, even "modern" in the literal sense of felt to be how to move forward in history. Again, this is not a war against modernity, as so many pundits have maintained. This is a war *about* modernity. Muslims require—and I believe they are constructing—Islamic understandings of how to live today that render bin Laden's politics a bad dream, and so his war the expression of a nightmare, evil and also foolish. We are waiting for a fifth fundamental understanding in the history of Islamic politics, and so yes, this may be a long war.

And just as obviously, efforts at direct intellectual engagement should be made. If this is a war of ideas, an essentially ideological struggle, then we should work hard to change minds. We should, in short, argue. But while argument, like violence, is necessary, one should not hope that argument—direct diplomacy—can solve the conflict, that is, win the war. As discussed in the preceding chapter, within the logic of Global Jihad, no argument is possible. (Don't listen to the devil and his lies.) And as a lawyer, I am sorry to report that even in far less polarized contexts, argument rarely changes minds in any fundamental sense.

The fact that no direct engagement—neither with bullets nor with words—with the enemy is likely to win this war does not mean that there is nothing to be done while we await Islamic ideological reform. If radical neofundamentalism must be supplanted in the minds of Muslims rather than defeated on the field of battle, then the fundamental political engagement must be indirect, that is, Islamist conflicts must be *won* outside direct confrontation with "the terrorists." Very few people are active members of al-Qaeda or any terrorist organization. The strategic question is whether people we call terrorists are respected, admired, their ideas espoused. The struggle for security is thus essentially a contest for the sympathies—for the political imaginations—of Muslims.

Precisely because our strategic interests are realized not against the terrorists but among the people, the audience, our response to Global Jihad should build on what we know about counterinsurgency.[3] We must, picking up on Mao's famous image, deny terrorists the cultural water in which to swim.[4] A retired general recently asked me: what about the 70 percent of Muslims who reportedly sympathize with bin Laden? That is, indeed, the point: what about the millions and millions of people for whom radical neofundamentalism provides an at least somewhat compelling account of their situation, and sometimes, a direction for violence? How one would measure either the depth or breadth of "sympathy" is unclear, but 70 percent of over a billion people is over 700 million individuals, dispersed worldwide—the "base" of al-Qaeda is potentially broad indeed. But it is among that population that real security can be established.[5]

How do we establish a secure political order? The same way we establish any other state of political affairs—by doing politics. Admittedly, it is easier to call for political engagement than it is to engage, but there is nothing magic or fundamentally unfamiliar about the problem before us. As suggested by Chapter Four, if we are to engage the world of terrorism, we must put aside some of the nostrums, prejudices, really, that we use to explain the world to ourselves. We must look, and listen, and think, and speak anew. Not because we know nothing—we know a great deal—but because we do not know everything. And if we wish to engage other people politically, it is critical, as discussed in Chapter Five, that we do not present ourselves as know-it-alls who have already diagnosed or solved "the problem," thereby casting people as historical actors, pawns perhaps, but not political allies or interlocutors. We cannot regard people with whom we wish to forge a global security order as puzzles to be solved (so they will go away). We must engage them.

To engage other people, we have to acknowledge their presence. Again, we may think of our fellow political actors, regardless of citizenship, as sharing the global stage—we are jointly producing a play. In so conceiving of global politics, we acknowledge the fact that other actors are living at the same time, like us, seeking ways to go on. As discussed in Chapter Six, in a very simple but serious sense, we are all moderns. Even neofundamentalists, whom we so badly wish to consider archaic, operate now, with a view toward the future—and this is the time of doing politics. Which is hardly to say that we all share the same goals or interests (there are conflicts in plays, too), but we cannot begin to do global politics until we address our fellow denizens of the planet. Even neofundamentalism presents a way to be modern, the topic of Chapter Seven. Although we are violently opposed to his suicidal modernity, it is a serious mistake not to acknowledge that bin Laden presents a modernity and that it has its appeal—and that appeal must be countered not among committed terrorists, but in the world.

While the world is large, it remains a shared space, again like a stage. As discussed in Chapter Eight, in this age of networks, terrorists, and assassins, it is too easy to forget that all politics is spatial, that the city (*polis*) is a place, and that the political question is always what kind of place will this city be? In promoting and maintaining a global security order, the question for people everywhere, not just in the United States, is what sort of order is the United States attempting to construct, to protect, and, perhaps most importantly at present, to promote? We are asking people to participate in an international security order that not only substantially expresses our view of the modern but that secures our privilege to deploy force. But ours is hardly the only way to understand the appropriate deployment of force—bin Laden has offered Muslims a very different vision, as discussed in Chapter Nine.

In trying to establish a global security order, we are asking people to imagine the stage, the globe, at least in broad outline, as we imagine it. In fact, we are asking them to share this vision of collective security and help us build it. In so asking for the participation of others, it is not enough to acknowledge their presence. Diplomatic thanking of allies is necessary but insufficient. We ourselves must be present. We must be, in short, responsible. This would seem to be simple, so simple—but how much of our security policy has been constructed in shadows?

We are asking people to share our vision of collective security to the extent that they trust us with weaponry. And to some extent they do: the rise of overwhelming military imbalance in favor of the United States has not occasioned the emergence of a new peer competitor nor even serious balance-of-power politics arrayed against us, at least not yet. But it is hard to reckon our security policy much of a success. Our plans for peace in Afghanistan and Iraq are being openly contested; bin Laden's story has gained credence; nuclear weapons are proliferating; emerging powers are acquiring arms of substantial quantity and quality. Perhaps most disturbingly over the medium to long term, we cannot be too happy with the help we have received in maintaining order: much of the world seems willing to let security be a U.S. problem, and it is—we are losing people and spending treasure at an appalling rate, but maybe the homeland is safer.

It is past time to ask ourselves some hard questions: How many of our actions are plausibly deniable? How often do we act through contractors, proxies, agents secret and not so secret but not us? How often do we consider killing an objective? How often do we kill by remote control, foregoing the opportunity for bravery and so respect? How seriously do we take responsibility for our actions? How strong a security order are we building?

CHAPTER ELEVEN

PEACETIME CONTESTS

War is preceded and followed by peace. A security order fails, and then there is war. The war is won and lost, and then there is peace, or at least order, again. War is thus bracketed by peace. If we add ideological substance to this chronological scheme, we may also understand the outbreak of war as representing the point at which a narrative hostile to the prevailing order became sufficiently compelling for people to take up arms. So, at some point, radical neofundamentalism became more compelling, at least to those people who became terrorists, than the existing security order, such as it was, and bin Laden's War began.

Viewed ideologically, the strategic interest of those fundamentally satisfied with the peace—those who do not wish to see war break out—is to keep the security order healthy by making it seem both foolish and evil to attack that order. The idea of radical neofundamentalism cannot be killed, but it can be made to look idiotic, unholy, or otherwise uncompelling, and hence militarily irrelevant. So how do we keep from becoming "the Far Enemy," as bin Laden has it?

As discussed in the preceding chapter, *indirection* is critical. It is very difficult for the United States to claim that "the security order that we have constructed and enforce is really for the good of all," even if that is true. But other people, who are not Americans, can make such claims plausible. Rephrased, other people should join us in maintaining the global security order, not only because they too benefit from peace but because it changes the character of the security order—it makes the peace international, rather than purely an expression of U.S. power. If the United States enforces the global security order more or less alone, then it does not matter much how well intentioned U.S. policy is: the security order, the *Pax Americana*, will be seen as an imperial peace.

Thus, while peace is, or should be, something that all of us—whatever our many differences may be—have an interest in creating and maintaining, the question arises: is the security order that we are trying to build attractive, something that others, especially in the Muslim world, would want to join?

The United States cannot deny, and often looks foolish when it tries to deny, that it is a great power, with a distinct culture and specific interests. It is true that the United States has marvelous traditions of tolerance and diversity and freedom, but Americans all too frequently take these liberal virtues to mean that there is no specifically American culture, and so others are wrong even to worry about the hegemony of U.S. culture and interests, and certainly wrong to be anti-American.[1] In short, Americans are wrong to dismiss worries about American imperialism. Only by overcoming legitimate concerns about American imperialism can we hope to get sufficient participation in a global security order.

Historically, the United States has rarely been imperial except in certain metaphorical, if important, senses. Even the great westward expansion and associated destruction of the native ways of life, justified under the doctrine of manifest destiny, was also a process of territorial limitation. Having seized the midsection of a continent, the nation essentially stopped conquering. Since then, the United States has won big wars, but time and again has gone home without annexing territory. The notable lost war, Vietnam, would have been at least simpler as a matter of conquest, and the current efforts in Afghanistan, Iraq, and Pakistan have been plagued with a sense that the United States will leave prematurely.

While it is true that America is a distinctive culture, it is also true that the United States is composed of many peoples, many cultures. So it matters that so many peoples have such large populations in the United States: Iraqis in Detroit; Afghans and Vietnamese in Washington; Jews in New York and elsewhere—just to name some recently belligerent peoples. The idea of a pluralist society ("melting pot" or "salad bowl" or what have you) is a cliché, and something of a sweet dream, but more of a reality in the United States than perhaps anywhere else on earth. The fact of pluralism, of diversity among our peoples, is critical because it gives the United States the opportunity to reassure those who would be our allies that space exists, that globalization is not another word for Americanization, and that women and men of good will everywhere should join us in constructing and preserving a peaceful home.[2]

But how, as a practical matter, are we to project ourselves, to woo the world? How are we to present ourselves so that others vouch for us, for our intentions, and for our commitment to global security? A few very basic and general things may be said.

1. *Diplomacy.* "Diplomacy" means much more than the formal etiquette that heads of state and their agents employ when dealing with one another. The American experiment has always been an experiment in political participation. The United States, a nation of lawyers indeed, has genuinely believed that we can talk, or sometimes write, ourselves into political community and even a just order. It has not always worked, but at its best, we truly have created one from many. As we seek to establish a global security order, this very American hope, that we may reason one another into a society of trust, is indispensible.

2. *Amity.* If a sense of the constitutional possibility of our joint action is the first requirement for a peaceful contestation of a modern security order, almost as needful is something intentionally informal—the creation of social bonds. We should do all that we can to encourage understanding among people, the purpose of public diplomacy. In the same vein, travel to distant places should be easy. Education of young people from such distant places should be supported, massively. National sports are an amusement and a social bond; international sports are also an investment in security. We must, whenever possible, make other people, however distant, human, and in so doing, make ourselves human to other people.

3. *Charity.* Development aid is not merely charity. But "mere" charity is a misnomer: charity has always been morally required of the powerful. It is literally a civilizing virtue, which is one reason the romantic tradition, going back to the Middle Ages, is important. Without charity, knights are merely thugs, not heroes. And we Americans are, by and large, a charitable folk. But from time to time, charity is not

the policy of our government, which claims to be putting the interests of Americans first. This is a grave misunderstanding: if we as a nation do not have the courage to be charitable, we are not worthy of our power—it is the duty of our government, which literally holds the keys to vast destruction, to be magnanimous, and—a word difficult to say in a democratic context—noble. To give.

4. *Helpfulness.* The global security architecture cannot work if people cannot participate in the global order, and therefore not only do not support it but see it as a plot against them. Thus we have medium- to long-term security interests in fostering development, not merely in the sense of alleviating poverty but in the sense of fostering self-sufficiency, and hence the possibility of commitment rather than resentment.[3] Charity, as such, is always only a temporary response, a gift but not a way of life for the recipient. As the old saw has it, give a man a fish, feed him for a day. Teach him to fish, and he feeds himself. As importantly for our purposes, our fisherman may become fond of the river where he makes his living. Global development is critical not least because it holds forth the possibility of commitment to a world order, a sense of the globe as home, worth living in peacefully and handing over to children, as opposed to valorizing their suicide.

5. *Self-discipline.* We should understand the establishment of a more participatory, and effective, global security regime as being worth substantial national effort. (As this decade of war has demonstrated, we certainly struggle when the regime fails.) Most of our efforts will be nonviolent but will cost money. Consider the imposition of trade sanctions, which often hurt both the sanctioning and the sanctioned country. Surely the United States has a profound interest in a free trade regime; at the same time, the restriction of trade may be one of the more effective means, short of violence, to get a government to change its behavior. Or consider the outright restriction of trade, notably arms. While the United States makes a great deal of money, and, perhaps more importantly, ensures the loyalty of our "friends" by selling weapons, insofar as we are serious about enforcing global security, we should stop selling so many weapons to so many people. And we should work hard to keep other parties from selling such weapons, too. Will this cost money, at least in the short term? Of course—people are quite willing to pay good money for the capacity to kill one

another. But increasing lethality in general will not be in the interest of global peace, and therefore not in our interest.

6. *Accountability.* If we wish other people to know where we stand, we must try to be open, to be knowable. We must understand that our collective, governmental actions are public by definition. We act; we are observed; and therefore our actions are also presentations. So if we hold a trial, the public, the global public, may ask: was it a fair trial? This is not to say that we can achieve complete transparency; no people is fully known, and we do not know ourselves all that well. Much of life—consider business or legal proceedings—requires a degree of discretion. Those things said, consider Guantanamo, the suspension of *habeas corpus*, the practice of rendition, the proliferation of wiretapping, the refusal to deny torture—the culture of secrecy that has sprung up in recent years. Despite much talk and some improvement under the Obama administration, too much remains shrouded. In what senses can this government, and therefore the American people, honestly be said to be open, knowable, present? Respectable?

7. *Hospitality.* Our sense of hospitality (or, in a different key, our national self-presentation) must be at least as good as that which we would expect of a new neighbor (or a moderately successful business). So, for example, our borders are not merely lines at which we define and attempt to regulate human migration; our borders are also points at which we welcome people into the country. Most of our points of entry, however, are less charming than a toll booth, if more pleasant than a prison: one is herded into a basement, shouted at, and generally reminded that this is a great country. This kind of thing represents missed opportunities for the United States to present itself, to be friendly.

In sum, in contesting what it means to be modern, the United States should self-consciously attempt to be

- Diplomatic
- Friendly
- Charitable
- Helpful

- Self-disciplined
- Accountable
- Hospitable

And what of the politics between war and peace, nation-building? If war is an effort to reestablish order, and therefore war is bracketed in time by a stable peace, then a war is truly over when those who had been enemies, or merely chaotic, have a society well-organized enough to participate in the international security order. The failure of foreign policy to preserve the security order, that is, the descent into war, thus implies an ascent toward a security order, commonly referred to as "nation-building." World War II ended not with the subjugation of places like Berlin and Tokyo but with the reintegration of Germany, Japan, and other belligerents into the community of nations, and in particular, into the security community.

"Nation-building" is a somewhat awkward, even misleading, phrase for many reasons. As recent history unhappily demonstrates, the institutions of a modern state can be established but cannot thrive or even survive if other aspects of social life, economic and legal institutions, ethnic and partisan identities, a degree of prosperity and a sense of community, education and more than a bit of hope, perhaps even pride, and so forth, are not functioning in reasonably healthy fashion. That is, the "nation" that must be built includes not only a functioning state but much more, a healthy *demos* in a sound *societas*, to mix languages. But we Americans tend to be rather inchoately democratic, and not that good at thinking socially, and so are discovering, much to our frustration, that nation-building cannot be done quickly or by mere application of expertise. A great deal of work must be done, over time, by the inhabitants of a place—they must come together, live together, work together. So the question for us, now, is, what can be done to foster a healthy nation? How should intervening forces with no desire for dominion, preeminently the United States, attempt to encourage the establishment of a viable nation, and thereby, a durable peace?

There are many things that external forces can and, at least in some circumstances, should do. Provide for basic peace and security. Ensure that basic elements of modern infrastructure (water, power, roads) are operational. Ensure the rule of law and the availability of a sound currency, and so forth—in short, help to provide a context in which life can be lived reasonably well, thereby giving people a stake in the peace, and a desire to keep it.

From this perspective, the logic of nation-building flows seamlessly from that of counterinsurgency (or, better, the other way 'round).

Understanding nation-building in terms of counterinsurgency also raises the major problem with nation-building in a painful way. Suppose the counterinsurgency fails to achieve its central objective of winning the hearts and minds of the people, and thereby their participation? Suppose, after major combat operations are over, that the intervening power comes to be understood not as helping to build a new nation but as an occupying power? Should the intervening power redouble its efforts? Or should it withdraw and rely on its ability to quarantine the situation?

As discussed, it would be foolish for me to attempt to answer, in the abstract, questions calling for particular political/military judgments. Even if we specify particular conflicts, perhaps Afghanistan or Iraq, or now, Pakistan, many others are in a far better position than I am to say whether our current efforts (or efforts we may yet make) have a chance of working in their contexts. Still, it may be useful to state a few general, and not entirely consistent, principles or lessons, most of which seem demonstrated by recent history.

1. Make gifts. Nation-building efforts should be presented as efforts to establish amity, friendship, among peoples and their representatives and to repair the damage done by war. Consequently, nation-building efforts should be, and should be perceived as, expensive and thoughtful. Anything less indicates a lack of seriousness on the part of the intervening nation, hardly a sound foundation for a partnership. And from our perspective, almost anything we might have given Afghanistan and Iraq at the close of major combat operations would have been far less dear than the blood and treasure we have in fact spent.

2. Gifts should be given on arrival. In both Afghanistan and Iraq, military victory appears to have been followed by a period of relative inaction and the gradual formation of an insurgency, so that safety actually decreased over time. Our political efforts only gained priority once it became clear that conventional warfare had failed. Had substantial, visible, concrete efforts to improve life in Afghanistan been begun even as major combat operations were ending, would the insurgencies have formed or gained such strength? Would we have more credibility?

3. Demonstrate the firm intention to leave. Having established its bona fide—literally, good faith—intentions, the intervening power should make it clear that it has no interest in owning or annexing the territory and will leave when circumstances, especially security imperatives, warrant.

4. Demonstrate the willingness to leave sooner rather than later. In determining the length of time to stay, security interests are decisive: since the intervening power has no interest in owning the country, it will only stay as long as, on balance, its presence in-country provides more security than its withdrawal. Establishing a security order is not a matter of winning a decision, as Clausewitz might have said, and, as insurgents know, abandoning territory is not necessarily a sign of weakness. Pulling out of Afghanistan, for example, might be wise: the question is whether a relatively isolated Afghanistan is safer, contributes more to the security order, than a counterinsurgency. Ideally, a peaceful nation with a well-functioning government will be established on the territory where there was war, and the intervening power should be prepared to expend considerable resources in achieving this goal. At the same time, a distant second best, containment, generally remains an option. Knowing this, the inhabitants must be forced to choose how they want to proceed.

5. Be willing to reengage. Containment is, by nature, a partial and temporary solution. From the perspective of the security order, the question throughout the period of containment is how to make the dangerous territory safe and integrate it into the security order. Thus, even when withdrawal and containment is the right decision, the intervening power should remain prepared to reengage, to try again when circumstances—and particularly the willingness of the inhabitants to work together and make peace—warrant.

6. The intervening power should recall that its in-theater actions will be judged, and therefore must be evaluated, in a global strategic context. Conflicts between relatively local and more global objectives are likely. For obvious example, an intervening power that withdraws will be tempted to use assassination to minimize security risks emanating from the abandoned territory. For reasons discussed, such a program is likely to come at substantial strategic costs.

As the foregoing list of lessons suggests, the term "nation-building" perhaps oversimplifies, by making the enterprise seem essentially local. While national participation is a *sine qua non*, the security that nation-building seeks to establish is not a local concept. Conversely, precisely because local participation is required, forging a security order must have local benefits. The establishment of trade, educational, and cultural links with the wider world are crucial to achieving prosperity, which is now defined globally (no modern society is anything like self-sufficient). Moreover, for the citizens of a war-torn country, taking advantage of such opportunities can comprise a peaceful future, an alternative to rekindling the war. Conversely, it must be broadly understood that such possibilities would be lost if the war were to break out again.

From a strategic perspective, however, the political order we are trying to heal is not, at bottom, the national order—it is the security order, which is an aspect of the global order. The question is not simply whether institutions in places like Cambodia, Congo, Haiti, Iraq, or Kosovo are functional in isolation. As Afghanistan before 9/11 rather conclusively demonstrated, we cannot really afford to have places completely outside the security order. The strategic question is whether such places can be integrated into, or at least contained by, the global security (and by implication, social and economic) order. The key analytic context, therefore, is global, not national.

This sense of priorities—that we are doing global politics first, local (social) politics second, and only then, third, can we hope for the institutions of the state, sets bounds to distinctly national projects. If the choice is to be made between the form of the nation-state and the safety of the people, the safety of the people must take precedence. If the choice is to be made between the form of the nation-state and the security order, the security order must take precedence. This is one of the meanings of the dissolution of Yugoslavia and may yet be the significance of Iraq. And if the choice is between the security order and local safety, the United States can be expected to prioritize the security order, that is, its own safety.

Nonetheless, from the perspective of the security order, and hence the fundamental strategic interest of the United States, the institutions of a functioning state remain essential. The construction of the peace after the war is only successful when the people are sufficiently autonomous that they may adopt, buy into, the security order and help to build the peace for themselves and for others. In consequence, the point of nation-building (as opposed to colonialism) is to foster the independence and autonomy (not dependence) required for active participation. Such broad collective action on the international stage—even under conditions of globalization—requires the institutions of the state.

Thus we can only say the war is finally won when a successful nation is constructed. The nation, in this view, mediates between its people and the global order. A successful nation both fosters and protects a civil society that provides a home for the people who live there, and constitutes a state that can represent its people on the international stage. Fostering the emergence of such nations, amid ruins, is difficult but not impossible.

CHAPTER TWELVE

WARTIME CONTESTS

Our current military operations signify in two connected but distinct realms. On the one hand, we have tried to use force to defeat our adversaries, those we believe to be terrorists or in league with terrorists. On the other hand, our efforts are significant primarily for a different population, the Muslim world that we require to find a modernity better than bin Laden's. While we are fighting "the terrorists," we wish to do politics in "the Muslim world"—and the terrorists are not the same as the Muslim world, or even the people of Iraq, Afghanistan, and so forth. Since the two populations are not the same, physical control over our enemies, which the exercise of force is supposed to bring about, and symbolism for those with whom we wish to do politics, or at least do not wish to antagonize, have been decoupled. Bin Laden's War is significant in part because of this decoupling between military force and political significance, which very roughly corresponds to the distinction between "tactics" and "strategy."

The terrorists are defined by the conflict itself, that is, by planning, committing, or aiding terrorist acts. Enemies are those individuals who have made themselves enemies. Obviously and not to mince words, to defeat or at least incapacitate such enemies is a military imperative. As discussed above, however, the enemy is also defined as those who have adopted and act upon an ideology, and because an ideology cannot be killed, it must be rendered uncompelling. But uncompelling in whose eyes? In the view of those who might become convinced by radical neofundamentalism or other violent ideology, and so take up arms, become a new generation of terrorists. Thus while an absolutely necessary and immediate struggle is with the terrorists, the more fundamental and longer-term struggle is with the ideas that impel terrorism. (As often as the phrase has been ridiculed, these conflicts indeed constitute a "war on terror.")

In contrast, in a traditional war, enemies were at least roughly defined by geography, prior to the outbreak of hostilities. Consider, by way of examples, Germans or Southerners, my stock. In fighting Germany and the South, places with people, geography could stand in for individual persuasion, much less action. Control of land was the name of the game, because it entailed control of the land's inhabitants. More specifically, we, the United States, determined to take Berlin and burn Atlanta; we demanded unconditional surrender of places and organized forces, assuming (correctly) that the people would follow. To be blunt, control of territory in Iraq and Afghanistan has not engendered the acquiescence of the people.

It made considerable sense for us to imagine World War II, or the Civil War, in military ways, as opposed to political ways. We were at war with Germany and the South, not Germans and Southerners. We had power, and at the end of the war, our adversaries were powerless. Our enemies were not participating in politics; they were not political actors. In this context, the feelings, beliefs, and so forth of enemy soldiers were not very important. Again, the situation in Iraq and Afghanistan is different.

From the traditional perspective, in which war makes politics irrelevant, it was a provocation for Clausewitz to say that war is politics with the addition of other means, a provocation that has generally received only lip service but that this book pushes hard: war is not only a political expression of the sovereign but is also doing politics with the enemy, even the vanquished enemy. What bin Laden has made clear has always been true: successful campaigns have always required the transformation of the enemies' world, which traditionally required the physical occupation of their lands and which in the present conflict evidently required the invasions of Afghanistan and Iraq. Invasion changed the meaning of the South and of Germany, and that was necessary because—absent a final solution—we have to live with Southerners and with Germans.

As has already been suggested, however, the present conflict is more subtle. Again, this is a struggle over the nature of modernity, a conflict in which the physical occupation of land is a perhaps necessary part but is largely a distraction. Most specifically, *this war is a contest, especially with those others who are neither citizens nor yet enemies, about the character of the global security order.* Radical neofundamentalism presents one vision of the current order. We must present a more powerful—not merely compelling, but attractive, and deeply legitimate—vision of a peaceful society.

As a practical, operational matter, however, it is impossible to contest "modernity" or "the character of the peace" directly. Militaries must take specific actions, which are unavoidably significant in multiple ways. In judging the wisdom of a proposed action, we are thus confronted with incommensurate, even conflicting, interpretations. What we do may mean more than one thing. In particular, the symbolic, strategic significance of an operation among the people we would impress may far outweigh its direct, tactical effect on the people we believe, to a moral certainty, to be our enemies. Albeit vaguely, the problem posed by this disjunction between strategy and tactics, between political participation and the disenfranchisement of coercion, is familiar enough, discussed under headings like "collateral damage" and "war in the media." This or that ugly incident is broadcast at some political (strategic) cost, even if the incident may have been tactically advantageous (a bad guy was killed). This common understanding, however, is a serious misunderstanding. The conflict is not between political interest and military expediency. The military is political by definition. The conflict is between tactical advantage (this battle) and strategic interest (the defeat of bin Laden's ideology in the world).

To make matters worse, tactical advantage will usually be relatively clear; strategic value will be impossible to ascertain with any precision. Much of our struggle with Islamist violence to date has been, to use an old phrase, penny wise and pound foolish, willing to win battles and lose wars. (The United States did not lose a substantial engagement in Vietnam, and the Soviets won almost all of their engagements in Afghanistan.) In many situations, however, tactical interests must be subordinated to strategic interests. This war is different from our prior wars because our military must learn to evaluate its actions politically if it is to achieve strategic success and hence security. *Recognizing that the tactical costs may be considerable, our strategy should be to fight our wars in such a way that we foster Islamic alternatives to radical neofundamentalism.*

What, practically, does this reassessment of this struggle mean for U.S. policy? There are three essential aspects to a successful strategy for winning the struggle with radical neofundamentalism.

1. We must live up to our own ideals.

This is a contest over what it is to live in today's world, which is to say, this is a contest over political ideals. Both the military and the law are deep wells for our virtues, but our recent practice has often strayed far from our preaching. For obvious example, we often espouse the rule of law, which of course requires fairness. Oftentimes, treating someone fairly means treating them on an individual basis. From this perspective, the mass detentions at Guantanamo and elsewhere have been disastrous in part because the United States is seen to be treating all Muslims indiscriminately (just as bin Laden says).

While Muslims themselves must develop a new Islamic politics, there are many things that non-Islamic governments can do wrong, in effect strengthening bin Laden's narrative. The United States, in particular, continually must be aware of the danger of playing the role of "enemy" in bin Laden's story and thereby precluding the success of other Islamic understandings of politics. Wars can be fought badly; reconstructions bungled; people tortured and otherwise abused; the religion insulted—lending power to charges that the *ummah* is threatened, that this is another crusade, and so forth. Even operations that may be tactically, locally successful can damage U.S. strategic interests by limiting the ability of moderate Muslims to refute simple conspiracy theories in which the United States is the Great Satan, which they must if they are to articulate an Islamically authoritative politics to supplant radicalized neofundamentalism. That is, if we are not careful we undercut our own story, and end up strengthening bin Laden's account of the world.

I emphatically do not mean to suggest any slackening of resolve on our part, indeed just the opposite. The Berlin Wall was built, and finally torn down, by the East. The West did not waiver in its conflict with Soviet Communism and certainly not in the conflict with Nazi aggression. Now, as then, our resolve must exceed that of our enemies, and it will. That said, our resolve is aimless if it does not reaffirm our ideals of who we are and how we conduct ourselves.

It is said that this is a new kind of war, and it is. But that this is a new kind of war does not exempt our own actions from scrutiny. The Civil War, World War I, World War II, the Korean War, and the Vietnam War were also, in their day, new kinds of war. The United States and its allies cannot play to bin Laden's script simply because he offers a new kind of war. Again, we are in a struggle over the character of the contemporary world. If we do not live up to our own ideals, then we and our ideals will not be taken seriously. We will be literally discredited, that is, no longer believed. It is worth remembering that the British took and held India for so long not by the force of their own arms but because they were utterly believable.

2. We should take responsibility—boots on the ground.

To understand power in terms of belief, to understand war to be political, means also that war is deeply human and must be waged first and last among humans. Since at least the Civil War, powerful elements within the U.S. military establishment have attempted to mechanize war whenever possible. Although mechanization generally has led to the increased lethality of U.S. forces, killing is relatively easy, at least for those with sufficient money and hence tools. But this is ultimately tactics, as Vietnam and other conflicts in which U.S. forces achieved a high kill ratio but did not achieve their objectives, should have taught us by now. Mechanized war, in which a force comes, kills, and leaves, tends to be unconvincing to those left standing, because such force is *politically* almost irrelevant. The fundamental distinction between enemy and ally, those who fight against us and those who fight with us, is rarely disturbed by mechanized warfare.

If we have learned anything serious about politics since 1914, it is that the successful conclusion of a war requires the forging of political bonds, which demands modes of engagement more profound than a video game. The significance of boots on the ground, as with cops on the beat, is that human presence changes the structure of local society. By virtue of superior physical force, new men and women take control in a locality, lead, and embody that responsibility with their personal presence. Society, the forms of human interaction in that locality, is thereby changed. (Consider, in contrast, the increasingly fashionable assassination by Predator drone.) Once a local society has changed, so has the range of political possibility. If the change appears to be durable or to cause other durable changes (the adoption of a new constitutional government, perhaps), then the inhabitants will learn how to act within the new environment. From this perspective, the very human tasks of what used to be called "empire" and is now "nation-building" are not more or less dispensable activities that come after military engagement. Political engagement is the only way to win even relatively local wars. Warfare is not only policy by other means: warfare is political before the conflict begins, during combat operations, and after the peace is made.

Understanding warfare as the conduct of our politics, for which we are inescapably responsible, affects how we work with other forces, and especially local forces. Alliances have always been a part of war and will remain so. Indeed, as we have seen in a number of recent conflicts, alliances (and the imprimatur of the UN Security Council) can contribute to the political legitimacy of a war effort, and hence may be of strategic significance even though operationally insignificant. More particularly, at certain times and places the interests of the United States may be aligned with the interests of specific local forces, and such forces may have a real chance of success (perhaps with U.S. help), and therefore local forces may stand in for combat that might otherwise be done by our military. The early stages of the war in Afghanistan, in which much of the work of overthrowing the Taliban government was done by the Afghan fighters of the Northern Alliance, might be viewed as an example of such a situation. While this campaign was hardly an unqualified success—bin Laden escaped, and both the Taliban and al-Qaeda regrouped—the example is enough to suggest that there are situations in which it is wise to use local forces. Finally, because the successful prosecution of the war requires the establishment of a durable peace, much work with local security forces ordinarily will be required, even when U.S. troops carry the burden of combat.

While working with other forces may be necessary or at least prudent, understanding our wars as politics for which we are responsible tends to discourage the use of allies, including local forces, *in lieu of* U.S. forces. Each of three reasons establishes a fairly strong presumption against fighting by proxy. First, uncertainty: in many cases, it will simply be impossible to predict, with any confidence, who is likely to succeed, and it therefore may be difficult to know whom to support. Second, local forces that can be portrayed as lackeys of the United States are likely to compromise or even lose their local authority. Third, and the fundamental point here: *to be credible, the U.S. must take responsibility for its wars.* Fighting by proxy, or by remote devices like drones, dilutes that responsibility in an existential sense, because U.S. lives are not at risk. The message we send through fighting by proxy is clear and politically weak. Thus a recurrent and difficult problem for the United States will be to find ways to cooperate, without being seen as avoiding responsibility.

But the United States has been at pains to minimize or even deny the political—in the broad sense of social—character of that willfully abstracted conflict, the "Global War on Terror." Much of the last administration's war was conducted through clandestine investigations, wiretapping and various forms of internal and external spying, torture and other forms of interrogation, and judicial and nonjudicial procedures, often not only closed to the public but in undisclosed locations or denied altogether. While security, diplomacy, and even legal process have always required a degree of discretion, in area after area, the U.S. government adopted, and the Obama administration has been too slow to abandon, a position of nonresponsibility. The United States minimized its involvement, while simultaneously (and truthfully) maintaining that it had security and other interests everywhere. And so the United States, in its shadowy absence but undeniable presence, has lent itself to conspiracy theories, to portrayal as the malevolent force behind the Muslim world's very real ills.

3. We should be patient.

People have to discover how they are going to live in this time true to their beliefs, that is, how they are going to be modern. Such discoveries cannot be made for them and will come when they come. Put directly, allowing Muslims to develop new forms of Islamic politics may require amelioration of certain demands dear to the hearts of Western reformers. Free speech is an obvious example of an area in which "what is modern" seems so clear. Perhaps coming to that belief, making that belief central to a politics, cannot be accomplished overnight. But this is just an example, another question to be argued and decided elsewhere. The preliminary yet important point is that we should be patient. After all, history has waited a long time for those of us in the United States and other Western countries to become (what we currently think of as) modern.

The fact of American projection of force, a fact that this book assumes as it analyzes and prescribes U.S. outlines for policy, inevitably raises the question of imperialism, namely, is the United States an empire? If so, one might ask whether (1) this is a bad thing (the majority, post-colonial, position), or perhaps (2) a good or at least inevitable thing (the counterintuitive, bad-boy position). Indeed, a hostile critic might read this book to advocate postmodern military imperialism, even though I think this would be a misreading and is certainly not my intention. (Unfortunately, however, authors do not control how their books are read!) But this is not the place to decide, once and for all, the extent to which the United States ought to be understood and discussed as an empire. What was once an interesting discussion has become rather hackneyed; the analysis has become too semantic. For now, it is enough to say that the United States will continue to project force outward and, indeed, to express a model of political and social life. Although I do not think that these more modest propositions are enough to qualify the United States as an empire, they are more than enough to cause us to ask what may be learned from other peoples—most obviously the British—who have frankly considered their politics imperially.[1]

For many working in the English and American tradition of humane letters, feelings about empire, and indeed about the culture that empire affords, are powerfully yet ineffably bound up with one's response to Rudyard Kipling. I do not propose to add a whole lot to what critics as deep as Orwell, Eliot, or Trilling had to say about the man's work—it is enough to say that these critics, each politically opposed to much that Kipling stood for, and each a finer and more powerful mind, at least in all the obvious senses, felt compelled to engage Kipling long after he was dead, his art dismissed as vulgar, his politics as, at best, Tory apologetics for colonial oppression but quite probably something much worse, a sort of beefeater fascism.[2] And yet, if we Americans at the beginning of the twenty-first century are serious about projecting force, and we do not allow ourselves the moral comfort of the external critic (the "liberals" whom Kipling despised and who are roundly despised today by many in the security community), then there are important things to be learned, again, from Kipling.[3]

Kipling may be easily criticized, but should not be simply dismissed as a mouthpiece for imperial power. Much more must be said, quite apart from the fact that the refusal to exercise power does not appear to be an option.[4] One thing to be said is that few men paid more dearly for their political enthusiasms: Kipling worked hard to get his otherwise disqualified son John into the Irish Guards. "Jack" was killed shortly thereafter in the very imperial insanity of the First World War. Kipling wrote the history of Jack's regiment and devoted much of the rest of his life to historic preservation. Tragic irony is encountered rarely, but here it is. Two more recent stories of politics and war: Andrew Bacevich, a historian, West Pointer, Vietnam War veteran, and critic of U.S. military policy, lost his son Andrew in Iraq.[5] And my college drinking buddy Thor Hesla—as it happened, we never grew quite close enough to be called true friends, though I liked him—an inveterate idealist, actor, comic, writer, and a provocative man-child, moved from doing development work in Kosovo to doing more of the same in Kabul, where at age forty-five he was killed by a suicide bomber in the Hotel Serena.[6] So yes, we Americans—like the Brits—find ourselves projecting force, with the sacrifices that entails.

And sacrifice for what? What are we contesting? Force projection is not too far from imperialism, of which Conrad famously wrote, "What redeems it is the idea only. An idea at the back of it; not a sentimental pretence but an idea; and an unselfish belief in the idea—something you can set up, and bow down before, and offer a sacrifice to. . . ."[7] For Kipling "the idea" is not only Tory pride in the British lion, but—and this is the part that is so easy for us politically correct liberals to miss—love. Kipling loved Afghanistan, where today the United States finds itself engaged. Of Afghanistan, Kipling famously wrote that "East is East, and West is West, and never the twain shall meet."[8] Standing alone, this seems to be not only a fairly accurate description of our conflict with the Taliban and al-Qaeda but, more generally, a counsel of despair. The world seems to be divided into us and them—a position made somewhat intellectually respectable by Samuel Huntington's *Clash of Civilizations* thesis, a book depressingly popular in the Middle East.[9]

But "The Ballad of East and West" is worth rereading: the poem's most famous line expresses a common prejudice that the poem, in its entirety, argues against. Kamal, an Afghan chieftain, crosses the frontier to steal the British colonel's prized mare. The colonel's son bravely chases Kamal back over the frontier and far into enemy territory, until the youth's horse founders. Kamal is so impressed with the courage of the colonel's son that he gives him his father's mare back and indeed sends his own son to serve with the British. "The Ballad of East and West" is a story of bravery, respect, and generosity.

Kipling ends his poem on a note very different from "never the twain shall meet":

> *But there is neither East nor West,*
> *Border, nor Breed, nor Birth,*
> *When two strong men stand face to face,*
> *Tho' they come from the ends of the earth.*

Bin Laden's War is really a struggle over what the Muslim world—which is also our world—will become. We Americans need to remember our virtues, bravery not least among them, to ensure that we act in admirable ways, ways worthy of adoption. Only then can we hope to welcome the sons of men who had been enemies; only then can the East and West meet with affection and jointly construct a peace. And only then will we have won our own struggle, the more fundamental meaning of jihad.

PART FOUR

INSTITUTIONAL REFORM

CHAPTER THIRTEEN

NEW WORLD SECURITY

The security institutions that we regard as normal, that seem to have existed from time immemorial, in fact were established in fairly recent history. In particular, the structure of our armed services, organized under a centralized and extensive civilian bureaucracy, dates from the years immediately following World War II. Specifically, the Department of Defense was founded in 1947.[1] At the same time, the Air Force was founded, as a distinct service, and the CIA was established.[2] In other words, one should not confuse the present structure of our security institutions with the role of the military in this nation's history. The U.S. Army and Navy are older than the Constitution; this arrangement of security institutions is younger than many people now living.

The security institutions that we have today were designed in response to certain problems that had arisen in our conflict with the Axis powers and to confront a specific threat, the Soviet Union and its ideology, communism. Whether or not our security institutions performed well over the ensuing years and with regard to various issues are questions that, for present purposes, may be left to the historians. What is beyond dispute is that the Cold War is over, that is, the strategic predicate for the way we constituted our security community no longer exists. It is not impossible, but it would be extremely unlikely, and incredibly lucky, if institutions designed for one set of circumstances, one kind of world, one kind of enemy, one historical age, were well suited to new circumstances, the next world, the next enemy, the next age. It seems reasonable to think that contemporary security problems could be pursued most effectively by institutions designed for the purpose. By the same token, the changes in our nation's circumstances—precisely because this is a new world, with new kinds of wars—make it reasonable to expect that the institutional structure of the U.S. security community needs substantial reform. At any rate, the question is worth asking: what would U.S. security institutions designed to oppose Islamist violence look like? More generally, what institutions are required to realize the security posture—the responsible construction of a global security order—urged in this book?

If we believe that a security order—the maintenance of which we call peace, the failure of which we call war, the reconstruction of which we call victory—is a political order, then our institutions should be designed for the conduct of such politics. But "politics" is a very broad concept. The character of politics changes with time and circumstances. The political imagination and operations that this age requires are different from those of the Cold War. To be somewhat more specific, the security politics that this nation must undertake—and for which national institutions should be designed—may be characterized by the three assumptions set forth in Chapter One. To recapitulate those assumptions, but now understood not as a description of the world in which we seek security but more subjectively, as guides for our own action:

1. *We must speak more compellingly in the Muslim world.* Much of the politics that concern us is conducted in an Islamic idiom, by people who think of themselves as Muslims. What constitutes true Islam, and whether this or that group of people are to be regarded as true Muslims, is hardly the point. The point is that the world that much security policy will have to address is Islamic.
2. *We should think, speak, and operate globally.* The context for security policy is essentially global. Location matters, but in complicated ways that are not necessarily apparent from looking at maps. In particular, it is difficult to remember that "international" means much more than "among nations." This does not mean that nations are unimportant. But it means that security policy, or more broadly, foreign policy, may not be understood as exclusively a matter of state-state relations. Al-Qaeda is not a state, nor is the Arab Street, but they are critically important problems for our foreign policy as it plays out across the planet.
3. *We must acknowledge and take responsibility for the fact that we are projecting force.* The United States rarely acts because it must do so in any

mechanical sense. The United States is a powerful nation. It does not merely respond; it does not merely defend. That is what it means to have power. These conflicts are not about "defense" in any concrete sense: only very rarely does our violence repel invaders from the homeland. Indeed, we have no—and for the medium-term future will not face an—enemy capable of invading the United States, as opposed to simply killing people.[3] Security policy for the new world should move from an often disingenuous reactive posture to a more honestly active stance. We should take responsibility for our actions if we wish our actions to be respected. And it is difficult to imagine others participating in, making possible, the security order that we are seeking to establish if they do not respect us.

The United States operates in a global context and has reasons both selfish and altruistic for establishing and maintaining a global security order. At the same time, the United States operates with a degree of autonomy and reach that no other state currently has. That is, the United States operates an *essentially national* security policy devoted to establishing an *essentially global* security order.

This is hardly the only way to imagine international security. Since the UN Charter in 1945, it has been hoped that "international peace and security" would be protected by the international community itself, under the auspices of the Security Council. But the overwhelming majority of military institutions—and virtually all real war-fighting capability—has remained organized by nation-states. As a practical yet profound matter, it appears to be difficult and unrealistic to ask people to make the commitments and sacrifices that serious military operations require, if they are serving something as abstract as the international security order. And so the United Nations finds itself regretting not only the atrocity du jour, but its own impotence, the fact that, so often, nobody steps up and ends such atrocities. As true and sad as this is, before we become overly pious about our inability to back up "never again" with real muscle, we should ask ourselves whether we would put our children on the line.

To claim that security remains nationally defined, even in an age of globalization, is not to claim that national security interests are self-evident. Indeed, in practice, it is difficult to ensure that security policy is formulated and executed in the national (republican) interest. Far too often, our security commitments express not the interests of the nation as a whole, those things that constitute us as a public, but the immediate concerns of the various services, the contractors who deal with the government, commercial and local interests of diverse sorts, ideologues, and of course the members of this or that people. Such commitments need not be made, and I presume are almost never intended to be, against the clear interests of the United States. But the sum total of the fractured politics that constitute the military industrial complex is often quite at variance with any reasonable understanding of the national interest. Checks are written on the national account, and we all pay accordingly. And so we have silly weapons, redundant programs, unneeded bases, embarrassing allies, and even wars fought at least in part because, by the time the situation received real publicly minded attention, we had become entangled. Achieving a foreign policy that represents the national interest, as opposed to a constellation of institutional interests, usually justified by fear mongering, is no small feat.

And so, for the foreseeable future, the task will be to establish a global security order, in which as many nations as possible participate, that is also in our own security interest. We must come to understand the global and the national interest in terms of one another, as intertwined rather than opposed.

What follows, in this Part Four, is a brief discussion of a plausible institutional arrangement that might more truly express and more effectively secure American interests in the world, and in doing so, help make the world a better—safer and more loved—place. The thoughts put forth here are hardly radical and, in practice, should foster a security policy that would be in many ways far more traditional than much recent U.S. policy. But this is indeed a new war, and as such, requires substantial changes in the nation's conceptualization of security, and hence prosecution of this struggle, and therefore institutions. Any politician with the gumption to try to reform the security community along the lines suggested here will recognize the obvious, that regardless of the merits of reform, such changes will not be easy to accomplish. Political change is rarely easy. More specifically, the changes argued for here will not come easy, because they run somewhat counter to long-standing, and in many respects laudable, American understandings of how military affairs are to be conducted. Rephrased, precisely because Islamist violence represents a new and important threat, our own thinking will have to evolve, which inevitably means that assumptions, norms, and even doctrines that have informed the conduct of security policy will have to be rethought, and in some cases modified or even abandoned. And that, it must be said straightforwardly, is not to be done lightly.

But reform is necessary, and not just because we are confronting a new world. We have already changed a great deal in response to September 11, although much of that change was presented as a *fait accompli*, not the product of republican deliberation. And much of that change has been bad. We have fought long, expensively, and ineffectively. We have tried to justify practices—torture, assassination, the suspension of liberties, the targeting of our citizens—that we once considered shameful, even illegal. The nation has lost respect across much of the world. Our history has other horrors, of course, and few if any of our sins are completely without precedent, but in the years since September 11, I for one do not believe we have acquitted ourselves well. This generation is unlikely to be remembered for its valor or even competence. Recovering our better, more honorable, selves will not be easy.

If we are to reform our projection of force into something better, even noble, we must not lose sight of the hard truth that the way we exercise force is, in fact, the policy of the United States, of all of us, for which we will be judged. We owe it to ourselves to ensure that our use of force is the true expression of our national selves and does not merely reflect the current opinion of our security bureaucracies, or worse, the logic of our enemies. At the same time, we must continue to learn how to fight in this new world. In short, we are called on to make difficult distinctions between what is essential and must be preserved, by force if necessary, and what we must change to defend what is essential.

CHAPTER FOURTEEN

THE DEPARTMENT OF FOREIGN AFFAIRS

We may understand foreign affairs, the way the nation represents itself to and upon the world, along a continuum ranging from the most amicable to the violently antagonistic, from friendships to wars. Clausewitz's core insight is that politics does not cease when war begins, it changes tenor: war is a kind of politics, namely one that involves organized killing. While Clausewitz was the consummate military professional, his argument is that war is not, from the perspective of the sovereign who asks where the nation is going (strategy broadly construed), its own topic. To some extent this idea of a continuum is implicit in the phrase "security policy," which encompasses a great deal of activity short of war. Maintaining a standing army, or developing an arsenal, are parts of security policy even if not war—and much of what the security community does, certainly anything labeled "deterrence," assumes or even threatens violence, but is not (yet) violence. Conversely, and as will be discussed in more detail below, much of foreign policy, especially for the United States, is devoted to maintaining the peace, security.

At the same time, we do make distinctions, and one important distinction is between war and peace. Organized collective violence and preparations for such operations are special forms of political expression. So the question arises: once we understand diplomacy and military policy to be arranged along a continuum, can we say anything further about the relationship between peaceful and belligerent forms of politics? Can we say anything general yet useful about institutional design?

The U.S. Constitution approaches the question rather straightforwardly: politics rules. As a matter of law, and as mentioned in Chapter One, the civilian authorities, representing U.S. citizens, have greater authority than the military. The Senate has the power to declare war, and the House, the power to fund it. The president, who is elected, is the commander in chief of the armed forces. This is, of course, only a beginning. While the subordination of military to civilian authority is a vitally important aspect of the frame of our government, the constitutional superiority of civilian authority to military authority, or for that matter, the normative superiority of peace to war, tell us little about politics during war. Sometimes peace fails, and war is necessary or at least unavoidable. What then?

Americans tend to "rally 'round the flag" in wartime, or, to use another cliché, to believe that "politics [meaning party politics] ends at the waterline." Americans who, despite this tendency, believe it necessary to criticize a war, for example, in Iraq or Vietnam, can point to the long tradition of political dissent. In this tradition, we have a democratic duty to voice (loyal) opposition to a bad war. We may even have a duty to refuse to fight, but waters grow murky here. Both those who rally 'round the flag and those who dissent tend, however, to understand war and peace as antithetical. That is, in the heat of argument during wartime, the idea that violence is a form of political expression, along a continuum with happier forms of expression, tends to be lost. That is, despite the U.S. Constitution and Clausewitz, military thinking and discourse tend to *supplant* political reason. Clausewitz was right, but his truth appears to be one of those truths that is hard to keep in mind (there are temptations here).

The security question that we should pursue, even under the pressure of being at war, is how does the nation's violent politics, both actual and threatened, relate to our peaceful politics? How, to put the matter structurally, does the diplomatic function relate to the military function of government? We may begin, with the Constitution, from the proposition that national military force is a means to an end—to protect, and serve, and even to sacrifice, if necessary, in order that the nation may live at peace. Moreover, security policy (the maintenance of huge standing armies, expensive alliances, the development and deployment of weapons we hope never to use) is all about keeping the peace. On the other hand, precisely because the United States finds itself establishing a security order, we may go so far as to say that foreign policy, diplomacy, has no more important task than the cultivation of a peaceful global environment. The purpose of war is peace; peace is preoccupied with the possibility of war.

The diplomatic and the military functions of government should be seen as dynamically intertwined. The foreign policy establishment must be given every tool to foster the health of the security order. This is discussed in a bit more detail below, but the basic idea is clear: the United States is not presenting itself within some preexisting security order, in which the United States engages in diplomacy and of course has the right to defend itself. The United States, for better or worse, finds itself as the principal (not sole!) builder and custodian of an order. For the United States, therefore, much of foreign policy is always already security policy—we have assumed grave responsibilities and must now try to live up to them. This is an expensive proposition.

Rather than simple war or peace, we now have—as we long have had—situations imbued with various levels of security, implicit threat, sudden terror, open hostility, and war. In such a world, diplomacy should be understood not in terms of its alleged opposite, "war"—are we ready to fight the Soviets at the Fulda Gap?—but in terms of establishing and maintaining a security order under varying levels of stress. Such diplomacy is suffused with the possibility, and sometimes the actuality, of violence. It is (or should be) the foreign service that will first recognize that threats are rising and that the judicious show or application of force may avert worse problems, that is, we may avoid a more profound failure of the security order.

By the same reasoning, the outbreak of war represents a failure of the foreign service; a situation has spun out of control, and military action is required. Failures come in various degrees, however. To say that the security order has failed to preserve the peace at this time and place is not to say that the order no longer exists. Most simply, the security orders with which we are concerned tend to be geographically vast, and collectively, global. Most combat, still, is very local. Localized violence is an insult to, but need not dissolve, larger security orders. Most European life went on normally while Yugoslavia disintegrated. The failure of a security order means only that violence may be required to restore peace. The outbreak of war/failure of a security order simply means that peace will not be restored without violence; what kind of peace, and so what kind of violence, make all the difference.

Even when a security order has failed, however, security remains, or should remain, a regulative idea. Although war is occasioned by the failure of order, the purpose of war is to establish order. War is remedial. In trying to fix something—from a car to a country—we have an idea of how the vehicle ought to function, how the country ought to be. By the same token, once we truly understand that the purpose of war is to create order, then we have a principle for organizing military policy: military operations seek to restore the security order.

We may understand this as a narrative, like a man riding into a deep valley or a canyon and then riding up the other side and out onto the plain. As conflict deepens, peaceful efforts at realizing vital interests are frustrated and too soon are acknowledged to have failed.[1] Since the interests at stake are deemed truly important, foreign policy moves toward more violent modes of expression. As the situation degenerates into war, military institutions take over, and conversely, more-diplomatic institutions recede from view. As the military conflict is decided, a new order is established. Nations are built; governments are established; alliances are forged. Peace reigns.

Foreign policy can never forget safety, and therefore violence. But conversely, the military's purpose is not to defeat or kill the enemy but to establish order. Violence may be necessary, but mere violence is simply a means to an end. Rephrased, mere violence is not enough to constitute a military *policy*. Violence, without more, is essentially irresponsible, because it does not confront the question: why is killing the enemy the right thing to do? How, specifically, will their deaths help to bring about peace? The horror of our involvement in Afghanistan against the Soviets was that we were utterly irresponsible; indeed, we took great pains to deny our involvement. Killing, evidently, was enough. Even though some of those Russian kids may have needed killing, to use the brutal Southern phrase, we cannot claim to be exercising a responsible policy unless we have much more to say about why we are killing and about how our killing is going to make the world a less murderous place.

Some red-meat critic may wish to argue that sometimes it is them or us, kill or be killed. In slightly more polite language, one might say that self-defense, and hence violence, is a sort of Darwinian first principle that needs no further justification. Those who are unwilling to be violent are eliminated by those who are. But the argument from coercion cuts both ways. In a situation of true self-defense, kill or be killed, one has no options, and therefore is not exercising power. That is, carried to the extreme, national self-defense is not a military *policy* at all. And such a situation, in which no choices confront us, is not our national experience and is, in fact, almost impossible for us to imagine. Our real wars have involved many hard choices. We have had, and do have, options, and the power to act in some ways or in others. We have had military policy. Whether we have had a *good* military policy is a perennial question for any nation that takes the exercise of force seriously, not to be avoided by hand-waving in the direction of self-defense. My red-meat critic is, at bottom, unserious.

We are now in a position to answer, somewhat more precisely, the question of the relationship between peaceful and belligerent forms of foreign policy. Foreign policy endeavors to establish and maintain a security order. *Peaceful forms of expression are intended to make violence unnecessary; violent forms of expression are intended to make more peaceful forms possible and even sufficient.*

Insofar as the Department of State is correctly named, it is too narrowly conceived, for at least three reasons.

First, the foreign policy of the United States is not exclusively concerned with relations with other states. Terrorists are not states. Nor is the Arab Street, nor the financial markets, nor any number of corporations, nor NGOs, nor supranational organizations like the World Trade Organization nor "the media," nor . . . the global stage is populated with any number of nonstate actors, and the United States, as a state, makes policy vis-à-vis these actors too.

If the first reason that "State Department" is too narrow a concept is institutional, that is, foreign policy is not just about states, the second is more functional, that is, foreign policy is not just about diplomacy. The United States projects itself through many different *kinds* of relationships. Most obviously, we have trade relations with most of the world. The Anglo-American tradition has a venerable practice of asserting that such relations are commerce and not politics. But if the United States has learned anything since it helped found the contemporary global polity after World War II, it is that commerce is politics. That is the meaning of the Marshall Plan, the Bretton Woods Institutions, and especially the web of contract and cross holding that does so much to constitute global society.

But if commerce is important, surely education is also very important? The United States dominates global higher education. And what about charity, development, and aid of various sorts, much of which is organized by the

U.S. government, but much of which is conducted by the American people? And what about military alliances or the flow of travelers for business and pleasure? All of these relationships create connections; foreign relations is much more than formal diplomacy.

Third, and most importantly, the United States is the to great extent unwitting builder of the global order, including the security order. The world as a whole, including the citizens of the United States, must also ask whether the vision of global security that the United States has worked mightily to establish and maintain is worthy of support. If the global security structure does not receive support both domestically and internationally, then the United States government cannot maintain it by force of institutional will, and the structure will fail. But if the security order fails (and in places it has, as in Iraq, or never really worked, as in Congo, or might yet, as in North Korea or Pakistan), then what? These are questions about world order and, constitutionally, our place and safety in it, not merely affairs of state.

How might we rename the State Department to signal our recognition of just how important its responsibilities are? Many countries have a foreign ministry. This is somewhat closer to the mark, but not as good as the traditional German (and before that, Prussian) name, the *Auswärtiges Amt*, the "outward office." In fine German fashion, that is too true but sounds too awkward in English. And besides, we Americans have departments, not ministries. So perhaps we should rechristen the bureaucracy: the Department of Foreign Affairs.

In keeping with this expanded conception of foreign policy, the Department of Foreign Affairs would be a larger and more powerful organization than the current Department of State. Recalling both the foregoing discussion of the relationship between violent and peaceful expressions of foreign policy and the earlier discussion of peacetime contests in Chapter Eleven, we may sketch the functions and responsibilities of the Department of Foreign Affairs roughly as follows.

1. *Diplomacy.* For reasons provided in Chapter Ten, more emphasis should be placed on traditional diplomacy. It is through diplomacy that we present ourselves, and so begin to do politics on the global stage.

2. *Civil society.* The Department of Foreign Affairs should pay much more attention to civil society than does the contemporary Department of State. Admittedly, the State Department traditionally has

paid some attention to "cultural affairs," and budgets for such things have recently been increased, albeit after years of cuts. But the traditional programs only scratch the surface of what ought to be done. Substantial resources should be devoted to nongovernmental institutions, to education, to travel—both Americans moving outward and foreigners moving inward—a central purpose of the Department of Foreign Affairs is to foster unofficial relationships.

3. *Charity.* Insofar as the United States is a great nation, it does great things, things worth recounting later. Precisely because we are powerful, we need to think magnanimously. Our generosity cannot and should not be divorced from our foreign policy—the Department of Foreign Affairs has a central role to play in coordinating the U.S. effort to be great among nations.

4. *Development.* The integrated global economic and security order that the United States is working to foster requires the participation of people around the world; development is a foreign policy and ultimately a security concern. Again, the State Department is not uninvolved with such development policies; and again, present efforts are too often understood as peripheral to the national interest, and hence are not as strong as they should be.

5. *Trade.* By the same token, the Department of Foreign Affairs should have far more control over trade policy than does the current State Department. Neither "commerce" nor certainly "homeland security" can be meaningfully separated from our foreign policy.

6. *Military affairs.* The Department of Foreign Affairs should have a much more decisive voice in military affairs than the State Department currently appears to enjoy. The Department of Foreign Affairs should be expected to ask the president for troops, obviously with the ultimate approval of Congress. At the same time, the Department of Foreign Affairs should expect to be called on by the military for analysis of the requirements for peacekeeping, demobilization, and similar tasks.

7. *Idealism.* At issue is whether the ideal of world order that the United States has worked to establish since World War II is viable. The vision is of a peaceful and prosperous world, in which peoples and individuals have great latitude to find their own way. Of course, this vision has been pursued unevenly and often to the selfish advantage

of the United States, and of course, the United States has sometimes failed itself. But such cynicism is all too cheap, and included here for balance and the comfort of a certain type of reader. The important point is that the United States not only represents, it has struggled to achieve, an idealistic vision. And as a matter of raw security, it has no real alternative plan: we are committed to a global, relatively liberal, security order. Security thus requires a foreign policy dedicated to making this vision viable, which means dedicated to convincing others to share our conception of a global security order in which happiness may be pursued.

CHAPTER FIFTEEN

THE DEPARTMENT OF MILITARY OPERATIONS

The Department of State is inaccurately named, but the Department of Defense is disingenuously named. The United States plays offense, not defense. It is true that, for several generations now, the United States has not set out to conquer foreign lands and incorporate them, and in this sense is not an empire. But it is more than a little misleading to claim, as we do, that we fight only to "defend" some preexisting set of interests. The United States has worked hard, and with considerable success, to establish a global security order. Relabeling the national effort to establish a security order a vital interest, and then characterizing the protection and extension of that order as self-defense, radically understates the magnitude of the enterprise undertaken by the U.S. security community since the end of World War II.

Here again history is instructive. The "Department of Defense" is a new name, adopted as part of the National Security Act of 1947, at the onset of the Cold War.[1] Until then, there were two military positions in the president's cabinet, the secretary of war and the secretary of the navy, each heading a department of the same name. As a phrase, the "Department of Defense" was somewhat ludicrous even in 1947: the United States adopted a "defensive" posture right after subduing much of Europe, Northern Africa, and the Pacific and while possessing offensive weapons of unprecedented power, soon enough to be deployed in a strategy of "mutually assured destruction." The best defense is a strong offense, indeed.

As the Cold War grew yet more serious, and wars by and with proxies were fought around the planet, the United States persisted in maintaining a "defensive" posture. As a nation, we appear to have needed to see ourselves as menaced. I do not say that the Soviet Union did not perpetrate great crimes. The Soviet Union was in many ways an evil empire, as Ronald Reagan put it with comic book clarity.[2] But the quantum of threat represented by the Soviet Union at this or that juncture is not the only point, or even the most important point, especially now that the Cold War is over and we are confronting new threats. Throughout the Cold War, the United States was, and we are now, engaged in the construction of a global security order. Profound questions of design, ineffable questions of participation, and vastly uncertain questions of long-term strategy abound. Such thinking is hindered if not precluded entirely, however, by claiming that this (a weapons system, the assassination of a foreign leader or maybe just a bit of torture, the bombing of a country) is necessary to defend ourselves. To state my thought very strongly: U.S. military policy has been, in a profound but literal sense, irresponsible. In thinking in terms of defense, we have tended to deny our own agency, and thereby our moral responsibility, freeing us to focus on what we do best, operations and tactics.

How might we try to reconstitute our security institutions to make them more responsible and thus more expressive of the national interest— including the national interest in constructing a global security order—and therefore more compelling, not only to U.S. citizens, but to others? Symbols are much of politics, especially in the military, and so a logical place to start would be with renaming the Department of Defense, as a symbol of our reimagination of its task and especially our renewed understanding of the gravity of the foreign policy we undertake through our security institutions. Moving away from "defense" would signal a superficially undiplomatic—but refreshing—candor about what the United States has committed to doing on the global stage.

In this time of institutional drift, it is tempting to recall our traditions and revive the old name, the Department of War. But War Department, as the agency inevitably would be called, is too narrow. Our world often calls for forceful expression short of war: protecting embassies, keeping peace, maintaining sea-lanes, establishing public safety after wars or riots or natural disasters, advice to fragile regimes, disciplining regimes that seem to be sliding toward tyranny or chaos, various activities conducted under the banner of "nation-building" . . . the list goes on, but the point is made. Too much of security is about capability and threat and military presence less than combat operations for "Department of War" to be a good name.

It is also tempting, and would be in line with the logic of this book, to merge the nation's security and diplomatic institutions in one grand Department of Foreign Affairs. We might imagine a single bureaucracy responsible for a unified foreign policy, modulated along the continuum between amity and violence. To recall the United States Seal, we might imagine a single agency charged with both the arrows and the olive branches clutched by the eagle. Despite its logic, however, a single organ for foreign policy, including military policy, is not a good idea. Most obviously, such an institution would be very unwieldy. Moreover, there are times—many times, in negotiation—when it is useful to have more than one party, an idea most familiar in popular culture as "good cop, bad cop." More generally, however, as every lawyer or spouse or member of a committee knows, much negotiation happens in the spaces among the parties. The institutions that conduct foreign policy should not be so unified that their room to maneuver is unduly constricted.[3]

Assuming that more than one foreign policy agency is necessary, then we must divide the continuum of foreign affairs (between amity and killing) at some point or points, and charge different institutions with different aspects of our role in the world. So how is the responsibility for defining the United States in the world to be apportioned? The natural place to break the continuum, the joint, is violence. Clausewitz never said that diplomacy and combat were the same. On the contrary, he said that each activity, each form of politics, had its own "grammar."[4] It would seem sensible, then, to divide bureaucratic responsibility for our role in the world between peaceful and violent activities, between the Department of Foreign Affairs and the Department of Military Operations.

A lot changed for the U.S. security community after World War II. First, the United States was openly engaged in building a global security order, most publicly symbolized by the creation of the UN Security Council. Isolationism was, if not dead, at least in full retreat. Second, the nation remained largely under arms. A partial demobilization was followed by the massive buildup of the Cold War, and soon enough the shooting wars of Korea and Vietnam. Third, the institutional structure of the security community grew much more complex. What had been essentially two services, the U.S. Army and the Navy, which had its own "corps" of specialized infantry, the Marine Corps, led—largely through the National Security Act of 1947—to a tangle of services and agencies, namely the U.S. Army, Air Force, Navy, a still not completely independent Marine Corps, and a host of newly and variously independent agencies responsible for "intelligence," most notably the CIA, along with a vast complex of private contractors. All this is, of course, an oversimplification, probably misleading.

As a result of these institutional changes, the U.S. security community is plagued with the sorts of problems that beset any large and relatively stable bureaucracy or group of bureaucracies, from General Motors to the State of New York to the academy. Fiefdoms develop. This is natural and to some extent unavoidable, a sort of institutional friction among the various components of the governmental mechanism that cannot be eliminated entirely, but nonetheless must be struggled against. The most obvious problem is sheer cost. Stories of wastefulness in military spending no longer raise eyebrows. But the problem is more serious, for a republic, than mere inefficiency: the interest of a part often effectively even if unintentionally takes precedence over the interest of the whole, the interest of the nation. The point is not to catalogue interservice rivalries (the topic is too vast and too familiar) beyond saying that the challenge for institutional design is to ensure that the interests of the nation are paramount.

It must be remembered that, historically speaking, the challenge is not perennial or even very old. While Army has played Navy in football since 1890, that rivalry is between academies, colleges. Through most of U.S. history, the military in peacetime has been a fairly modest affair. When the Civil War began, as Grant's *Memoirs* tell, we "called up" troops.[5] The armies that fought our bloodiest war did not exist, or hardly existed, when the war began. Those armies took shape during the course of the war itself. And after a war was over, the United States traditionally demobilized. In that context, interagency rivalry is hardly a concern. Real interagency rivalry, with its cost and distraction from the national interest, is a function of the vast size of, and consequent institutional divisions within, the durable bureaucracies of today's security community.

It also must be stressed that this is a question of institutional design, not morality. I would hope that nobody intentionally would favor the interests of their service over that of the nation; I am not talking about disloyalty. But people do tend to conflate their service and its interest with the national interests. It is easy and not wrong to think that the national interest is vast and amorphous, and it tends to be somebody else's job. In contrast, what members of the security community actually do on a day-to-day basis is usually very well specified and is, in fact, their job. And besides, the institution in which they serve (whatever it may be) was established to further the national interest, so that anything that benefits the service must benefit the nation. Thus, as a psychological and institutional matter, the consideration of the national interest—how should we as a nation, not we members of this or that service, act—is abstracted, postponed, less well done than the pursuit of narrower institutional interests.

What can be done to guard against this problem, which, it must be repeated, is structural, a function of working through multiple institutions? The superficially obvious answer is to unify agencies. One could imagine a single, essentially unified, Department of Military Affairs. Indeed unification was the congressionally stated purpose of establishing the Department of Defense, with the joint chiefs of staff reporting to the secretary of defense. But there are strong objections to excessive centralization, particularly in the military context. Most obviously, specialization has its role. As importantly, *esprit de corps*, and therefore tradition, is important. Even the Army/Navy game matters, in its way.

So how to reduce interagency friction without undercutting *esprit de corps*? More deeply, how do we foster broad understanding and intense focus on national military policy, as opposed to the mission of one's own service? Some progress has been made, notably under the reforms of the Goldwater-Nichols Department of Defense Reorganization Act of 1986.[6] Today's armed services routinely share personnel. This is a good practice, and even, as one moves up the chain of command, required. Within the army, the idea of the "general officer" (hence the rank of "general") is of a commander who understands the various aspects of a campaign, the uses of infantry, cavalry, and artillery; the requirements of transport and logistics; and so forth. Under

Goldwater-Nichols, for promotion to the rank of general or admiral, a commander is required to have served jointly with members of another service.[7]

But there are reasons to believe that such measures have not gone far enough, and that our security policy remains overly influenced by the parochial concerns of the security establishment. If we were really serious about fostering a truly national, rather than institutional, perspective in our military, we would simply abolish the upper ranks within the services, and make appointments in the Department of Military Operations.

Enough of structure; on to substance. Running a responsible military policy, and confronting radical neofundamentalism in particular, requires the United States—and especially its voters and taxpayers—to change its understanding of how the nation's military affairs are to be conducted. The United States has a long and very substantial military tradition, and this is a time of change. Some aspects of our military tradition are being renewed, and others reformed. As of this writing, many necessary changes are under way in the actual conduct of our operations, especially in Afghanistan and Iraq. The new counterinsurgency field manual is a big step in the right direction.[8] Much, however, remains to be done. The shift in our understanding of military policy should be articulated in more general terms, so that we may lift it from the tactical and operational level, the domain of military professionals, to the level of public and democratic discourse, where it may be used to judge the effectiveness of our security policy writ large, and so a critical aspect of our government.

There is an enormous amount to be said, but for present purposes, the transformation in our military tradition can be discussed under three broad headings: (1) the politicization of security; (2) the role of economic power, including technology, in securing national security objectives; and (3) casualties. Changing the tradition in these areas is by no means easy, not just because change is almost always hard but because there are very good reasons for the status quo. The United States has won almost all of its wars; its military traditions have in the main served the nation very well. Changing those traditions, then, is not something to be undertaken lightly. Nonetheless, sometimes the world changes, and the way we fight, think about fighting, and judge our government's conduct of our violence must change, too. While the obstacles to necessary reform are substantial, they are less daunting than they may initially appear and are certainly not insuperable.

The Politicization of Security

This book has argued that strategy is inherently political and never more so than in the conflict with a decentralized ideology like radical neofundamentalism.

Against this proposition, it may be urged that the role of the military is to defeat enemies, win wars, and defend the nation. Other agencies of the government—the political branches—are constitutionally required and, in fact, better at politics. Indeed, analysis offered in this book has more than once met with substantial agreement from military professionals, coupled with the objection that since the argument is essentially political, it is the responsibility of political decision makers, elsewhere.

I have considerable sympathy for this rather too-professional position. It is certainly true that the civilian control of the military is essential to the well-being of the United States. We do not wish the military to decide that it is the final arbiter of politics. This country, for all the strength of its armed forces, has never had a coup. The military's cheerful acknowledgement that it serves civilian authority is one of the proudest aspects of our military tradition.

It must also be said, however, that the argument that "politics is not our job" can be made to prove too much.

First, nobody denies that ultimate command over the military rests with the political branches. But the different jurisdictions and responsibilities of government organs should not be used as an excuse for limiting the thinking of public servants, even those who serve in the military.

Second, as this book has tried to show, so-called political questions are central to the formulation of strategy in current and imaginable conflicts, and are therefore relevant to operational planning, and even to tactics. For obvious example, the reactions of various sectors of the Iraqi population to the U.S.-led invasion and subsequent actions, such as the failure to prevent rioting, raised "political" questions of great military importance. Political questions are inescapably part of building a global security order. For success, we need others to participate, which means that the security order needs good politics. Simply declaring certain questions to be "political" does not magically make them "nonmilitary." Rephrased, the military must learn to evaluate its own actions politically to understand their strategic significance.

Third, all agencies of government, including those of the security community, quite appropriately participate in the formulation of the policies that they are charged with realizing. Aiding the formulation of national strategy has always been a responsibility of the security community. Under present circumstances, developing a prudent security posture simply requires numerous essentially political assessments. While the political assessments of military agencies should not be controlling (any more than the assessments of the Securities Exchange Commission control financial market policy in the United States), that does not relieve the security community of the obligation to make such assessments, and to evaluate their own actions in light of such assessments.

Fourth and finally, bureaucratic institutions often claim that politics, or responsibility, lies elsewhere. This claim is often convenient, and so should be treated with skepticism.

The Role of Economic Power, Including Technology

At least since Grant hammered the South—taking casualties but also causing losses he knew his adversary could not replace—the United States has achieved critical military objectives by harnessing the superior power of the U.S. economy to its war efforts.[9] In particular, the American talent for technological innovation has long benefited our military. Conversely, security interests have spurred technological innovation: the government funds research and buys advanced products. Most recent efforts at reform of the military have been premised on the proposition that security is to be achieved by intensifying the role of technology in the military.

If wars are understood politically, however, then the strategic question posed by a technology is how does the technology affect the polities in question? The materialism, often facile, that runs through our military tradition and that has animated most recent reforms of the military is simply inadequate to confront this question. Successfully deploying a technology for the assassination of a terrorist, for example, signifies tactically—the terrorist is dead—but how that assassination will affect security is a very open question. Conversely, for an adversary committed to the idea of an army as an organ of the state, for example, the Germans in either world war, defeat of the army represents defeat of the state. But as should be clear by now, neither the state nor an army are required for collective violence, and technologies that incapacitate states or armies may or may not thereby end wars. Vis-à-vis the

Confederacy, the Germans, or the Soviets, all of whom predicated their politics on the state with its vulnerabilities, the material power of the United States was convincing (most obviously against the Soviets, against whom the material power was not, after all, exercised). But in hindsight, the critical strategic point was that the adversaries of the United States were convinced of U.S. power, not simply that the United States amassed a certain amount of military capital.

Other combatants in other wars have not been so convinced. Possession of better technology did not decide the outcome in our favor in the Vietnam War, and as of this writing, has not decided Iraq or even Afghanistan in our favor. A politically more sophisticated analysis of the military significance of economic power and technological superiority would begin by asking how such advantages are likely to play out in a given context. It cannot be presumed that technology matters very much. In today's world, technology is ubiquitous and necessary, and therefore, often rather insignificant in the literal sense of not very meaningful. This does not mean that technology will go away. Presumably combatants will continue to employ the technologies available to them, as combatants always have. Al-Qaeda uses many of the same technologies as its targets. In the struggle with the ideology of radical neofundamentalism, technology is everywhere and appears to be irrelevant to the decision, because the conflict has not been joined in a way that allows for technological resolution. At present, there is no reason to believe that merely buying better technology will hasten victory.

One might generalize this point in terms of the argument of this book. To understand war as a matter for technological resolution is to understand the conflict objectively and tactically (how are these objectives to be achieved?) rather than subjectively and strategically (what sort of security arrangement may we reach together?). To understand one's enemies as the objects on whom military, technological, or economic power is exercised may to some extent be unavoidable—they are enemies—but it is not to understand the enemy as a political actor, even though the point of strategy is to transform the politics of (the surviving) adversaries. Thus the technological bias in American security thinking tends to hinder strategic political thought.

There are reasons, some good, some bad, for this technological bias. As noted, the U.S. military has won major wars by exploiting its economic superiority. Moreover, an objective and tactical approach fits well with the self-understanding within the professional military, in which politics is done elsewhere and doing one's own job well is rewarded. For their part, the military industries sell technological solutions because that is what they have to sell, and there is money to be made. In short, the technological bias of the U.S. military runs deep. For present purposes, however, it is enough to recognize that we have a profound bias, and that bias clouds the national judgment. Although there are signs of progress in the most recent budget, as a nation we keep buying weapons for which there are no adversaries, rather than, for example, employing translators.

Given the great wealth of the United States, it would be nice if security could simply be bought. But this is not the case and probably cannot be, as Thucydides and much more recent history remind us—our position entails danger, in no small part because of our wealth. Just as buying an infinite number of hammers will not design us a house, in securing the global environment in which the United States operates, it will not be enough to shop for high-tech weaponry (tested away from people in some desert) and elite soldiers. Instead, we need to present ourselves in the cities, make our case.

Casualties

From the perspective of orthodox security thought, the policy realignment proposed in this book presents a third fundamental problem: if taken, the approach suggested here is likely to result in higher casualties, at least in the short term. This book has argued that warfare is political, and that politics requires personal engagement, that is, our people need to be close to their adversaries—hence "boots on the ground." And, under the leadership of Generals Odierno and McChrystal in Iraq and Afghanistan—and the entire wave of military reformers led by General Petreaeus—the military has indeed adopted more humanly engaged tactics, with some promising results. This book has also argued that not only is technology unlikely to be decisive but it is something of a distraction from the real question of building safer politics. But, it should be objected, our personnel who are close to their current or recent enemies are vulnerable. By the same token, a major if hardly the only reason for the U.S. emphasis on high-tech warfare is that it keeps U.S. personnel safe.[10] And, at least since the Vietnam War, it is widely argued that American people have little stomach for casualties.

I find this argument powerful. Some military personnel with whom I have discussed the matter, however, have been less impressed. Casualties, I am reminded, are an unfortunate part of the military enterprise. Indeed. I prefer to think that a more engaged approach to our wars will allow us to construct a stronger, safer peace, and that our enhanced credibility will deter other wars and make terrorism less appealing, and that we all, whatever our citizenship, will be more secure in the medium to long run.

CHAPTER SIXTEEN

THE REINTEGRATION OF INTELLIGENCE

INTRODUCTION:
THE NEED FOR MORE SERIOUS REFORM

Before I get around to the real argument of this chapter, that the CIA ought to be abolished, and its useful personnel and functions reintegrated into the organs of government responsible for foreign affairs and military operations, let me be clear about what I am *not* arguing.

I have no wish to deny that many men and women serve the CIA and other intelligence institutions with great zeal and dedication, and sincerely believe that in doing so, they are helping their (our) country. But for purposes of political argument and particularly institutional design, the zeal and even morality of the individuals involved is not decisive. After all, one could say that many members of the *Wehrmacht* served their institution with the utmost zeal and dedication, and in the sincere belief that they were helping Germany—hardly an argument for German military policy circa 1939. This, indeed, was one of Niebuhr's central themes: the morality of organizations is not the same as that of individuals.[1] But good or bad, the morality of individuals in the CIA is not my point.

Nor am I denying that political enemies, and even real evil, exist in the world, and that sometimes force and even deception must be used. Force, it has been pointed out since Sun Tzu, can be greatly magnified by intelligence.[2] This is perhaps particularly so in modern ages, in which military operations are highly dependent on planning and communication, secrets that can be intercepted or stolen.[3] More generally, governments, like most human associations, require some secrets and therefore discretion. And where there are secrets, there are likely to be spies. As the old joke has it, if prostitution is the oldest profession, spying is a close second. (Perhaps "spying" ought to be changed to "private investigation," but never mind.) So I do not claim that the United States should do without intelligence services, at least not before the lion lies down with the lamb.

Nor is this the place to assess how the intelligence community, and the CIA in particular, has performed in the modern era. Much is classified; histories abound; and assigning blame and praise in specific cases would bog us down. I do not mean to be coy. My general opinion of the record and even competence of our security institutions is quite negative. But this book is not yet another lefty critical analysis of how the Cold War was prosecuted or even a discussion of whether our sins are somehow forgivable in light of the evils perpetrated by our enemies.

The question here is: should the US intelligence services, specifically the CIA, be radically reformed, and if so, how? With September 11, bin Laden has already raised this question more compellingly than I ever could. In 2003, we began a full-scale war in Iraq substantially on the basis of what might most charitably be called intelligence so very faulty as to form the basis of delusions or lies, a distinction that can be left to historians with a moralistic bent. (A little knowledge is a dangerous thing indeed.[4]) Meanwhile, our intelligence agencies have proven incapable of locating bin Laden. It's not that we have not tried: we have tortured folks, incarcerated people without legal rights in facilities whose existence we deny, and when necessary, we have used corporate jets to fly people to countries where they really play hardball. But so far, no luck.

After we had, in the 9/11 attacks, what was widely called "another Pearl Harbor" (the CIA was founded to prevent "another Pearl Harbor"), Congress and the president established the bipartisan National Commission on Terrorist Acts upon the United States (9/11 Commission). In July 2004, the 9/11 Commission released the 9/11 Commission Report, suggesting reform of the intelligence services. The Intelligence Reform and Terrorism Prevention Act of 2004 was signed into law in December, largely implementing the commission's suggestions, or at least promising to implement them.[5] So the question at issue here may be rephrased: did the Intelligence Reform and Terrorism Prevention Act sufficiently reform our intelligence services?

In its report, the 9/11 Commission maintained that intelligence services suffered from a lack of communication.[6] Rather than share information about al-Qaeda, intelligence agencies functioned as "stovepipes," in which information was passed upward within the hierarchy of the agency in question. As a result, information gathered by different agencies was not synthesized, and the significance of information was overlooked. The 9/11 Commission therefore proposed what amounts to a czar of intelligence, the director of national intelligence (DNI), a proposal enacted into law within the year.

In seeing institutional centralization as the key to improved intelligence and so security, the Intelligence Reform and Terrorism Prevention Act of 2004 resembles the National Security Act of 1947; essentially the same arguments were made for the creation of the director of central intelligence (DCI) as were later made for the establishment of the DNI. The 9/11 Commission contended, however, that the old structure failed to achieve its objective of effectively integrating the intelligence agencies. The DCI simultaneously was (1) directly responsible for an agency (the CIA); (2) supposed to coordinate activities of, and integrate the information produced by, other, competing, agencies, over which the DCI had little direct power; and (3) supposed to present daily security briefings to the president. In short, the DCI was wearing too many hats. The Intelligence Reform and Terrorism Prevention Act, therefore, made the DCI the director of the CIA, that is, a director of one agency among others, and transferred the DCI's other responsibilities to the DNI.

At least with regard to the failures of the intelligence community, the legislative response to September 11 was orthodox enough, but was the reform sufficiently thoroughgoing? The political need to take action quickly may have left insufficient time for a more fundamental rethinking of the policy goals at issue, and how best to achieve them. The Intelligence Reform and Terrorism Prevention Act proceeded on the convenient presumption that our intelligence failures, including 9/11, were merely repetitive accidents of bad leadership, ordinary incompetence, and a certain lack of institutional cooperation in what are admittedly difficult tasks.

In January of 2010, shortly after the Fort Hood massacre and the discovery of a known terrorist sympathizer with a bomb on board a commercial jetliner, President Obama took responsibility for intelligence failures, and promised to streamline the sharing of intelligence. In May of 2010, Faisal Shahzad parked a bomb-filled Nissan Pathfinder in Times Square. Later in May, Thomas Kean and Lee Hamilton, formerly chair and deputy chair of the bipartisan 9/11 Commission, testified to the House Homeland Security Committee about the government's failure to carry out many of the recommendations that emerged in the wake of the September 11 attacks, including the creation of more effective ways to share intelligence.

It is worth considering, at this point, whether something is more drastically wrong with our intelligence organizations, something that requires a more intellectually thoroughgoing response. It is worth thinking seriously about the possibility that the CIA has failed regularly throughout its history, and even if reformed as proposed, our intelligence institutions will continue to fail, because our security institutions are simply badly designed, fundamentally misconceived. To that end, this chapter argues that the existing model for the CIA is both wrong for its mission, especially in the contemporary security environment, and fundamentally un-American. While it no doubt has some benefits, the Intelligence Reform and Terrorism Prevention Act perpetuates the flaws of the existing paradigm and is, therefore, an inadequate response to bin Laden and inadequately provides for the security needs of the nation more generally.

CONCEPTUALIZING INTELLIGENCE

We might begin thinking about the reform of the intelligence institutions by sketching, in simple language but at a fairly high level of abstraction, the prevailing intelligence paradigm.

Intelligence is widely assumed to be "an asset," that is, a thing of value. We may even think of it as a form of intellectual property, like a trade secret, for example, the formula for Coca-Cola. Assuming that you wish to make Coca-Cola, then you need to know how. In pure accounting terms, such know-how is an asset. Simply knowing how to do something, however, will not give one an advantage over other parties who also know how. The formula for Coca-Cola has substantial economic value in a competitive market for soft drinks because other companies do not know it. Therefore, Coca-Cola keeps the formula secret. Insofar as consumers demand "the real thing," then Coca-Cola has a privileged position in the market for soft drinks. So, to generalize, when we speak of a trade secret (or intelligence) having value, we imagine (1) a competitive context, in which parties struggle against one another; (2) an information asymmetry, in which some but not all parties control valuable information; and (3) parties that seek to maintain or undermine that asymmetry. We imagine a world of competition over valuable secrets.[7]

Roughly this view of intelligence made a significant if limited amount of sense during the Cold War. In a world with a well-defined enemy, whose ultimate motive was known even if its tactics were sometimes opaque, the "national interest" was relatively clear. The Soviet Union wanted to hurt the United States, worldwide victory of the international proletariat and so forth, and therefore the United States wanted to hurt the Soviet Union. Assets could be defined in terms of that polarity. More specifically if not more sophisticatedly, information that could hurt the Soviet Union was an asset; information that prevented the Soviet Union from hurting us was also an asset. And, since the Soviet Union was trying to secure what it considered to be assets, too (through espionage), anything that the United States could do to thwart such efforts furthered U.S. interests (counterespionage). This gave rise to endless subtlety, and the genre of the modern spy novel, but the important point is that "intelligence" was defined in terms of a competitive context, the Cold War, that was essentially unquestioned. In that unusually determinate context, information asymmetries were valuable, secret, and sometimes worth killing.

While the pervasiveness of the East/West conflict meant that anything that could be done to advance our side, or hurt the other side, was a good idea in principle, in practice, direct conflict had to be avoided for the simple reason that both sides had nuclear weapons. Therefore, both sides expended a great deal of energy hurting "their" allies and protecting "our" allies, however unsavory ("he may be a son of a bitch, but he's our son of a bitch"[8]), as secretly as possible. And so was born a whole world of violence by proxy, of covert operations in which we denied all involvement. This was not merely a matter of institutional practice. In 1948, Eisenhower signed secret directive NSC 10/2, which "supplemented" the "overt" activities of the United States abroad with "covert" activities. These activities were to be conducted in such a way that if they became known, "the U.S. government can plausibly disclaim any responsibility for them."[9]

Intelligence and covert action were thus defined by our version of what Kipling, in *Kim*, called "the Great Game," a game that, like all games, had to be assumed in order to be played. Once we assumed we were engaged in a violent, perhaps existential, contest with the USSR and its allies (and there were lots of reasons to do so), then intelligence and covert action that could hurt the Soviet Union became objectives in both senses of the word: they were facts, and they were facts worth struggling to bring about, objectives to be achieved. As with any other such objective, expert bureaucracies could be established to manage intelligence and covert activities. Just as one might establish a space agency or a bureau of economic advisers, one might appoint a group of professionals, "intelligence experts," to gather and analyze intelligence by various means, and plan, pay for, and occasionally staff covert activity. This, indeed, was the natural thing to do for the government and the generation that had battled the Depression and then the Nazis in no small part by forming large bureaucracies, as the architecture of Washington, D.C., attests. And so, shortly after World War II, we first saw the establishment of a peacetime, independent bureaucracy for intelligence, the CIA.[10]

From its inception, the CIA has understood itself—and is statutorily defined—as apolitical. Section 103 of the National Security Act of 1947 made the DCI responsible for providing national intelligence. Subsection (2) states, "Such national intelligence should be timely, objective, independent of political considerations, and based on all sources available to the intelligence community." But this is not merely legal verbiage: the idea that intelligence is about facts is deeply engrained in the security community. Politics is for politicians; the CIA is a professional organization.[11]

The structure of the paradigm is now evident: (1) In a world of antagonism, even in peace, (2) the logic of fear rules. Since we know that the enemy is trying to hurt us, we must try to imagine how, so that we may gain information or otherwise act in order to preempt, prevent, degrade, or at least counter those efforts. (3) Our ability to defend ourselves from, and to hurt, the enemy is enhanced by secrecy, either to preserve or defend an informational advantage, or because we do not wish to engage in direct conflict. (4) Since the animosity of the enemy is presumed, intention is hardly at issue and information about, communications of, and actions by the parties may be treated objectively. (5) Since intelligence and covert action are essentially objective enterprises (points in a game), the enterprises are properly carried out by professionals and insulated to the extent possible from politics. (6) Since intelligence and covert activity are distinct from politics, neither the CIA nor other intelligence organizations are political organizations.

TRADITIONAL CRITICISMS
AND DEFENSES OF THE CIA

Criticisms

The CIA is ineffective. As noted above, since the CIA was established, the agency has been criticized, and defended, in ways that have become very well rehearsed. Critics have charged that the CIA is ineffective, that it does not advance the national interest. Such criticism has been made in two fundamentally different ways. First, the CIA has often known little about the world, and much that it has claimed has proved to be wrong. Time and again, the Central Intelligence Agency has simply not been very intelligent. Second, surely the national interest cannot be divorced from legality and morality, and the CIA has been accused, by any number of more dovish critics, of undermining both. In this view, the CIA is ineffective even when most (superficially) successful, notably in overthrowing foreign governments. There is a considerable literature here, much now backed by declassified documents, and for present purposes, it suffices to sketch the structure of the argument.

The CIA's mandate and activities violate core American political values. Criticism of the agency's lack of effectiveness shades into a more fundamental charge, that the agency is essentially un-American. A hierarchical and elitist secret agency, using uncounted tax dollars to operate largely outside the law, is hardly an expression of the values on which this democratic republic claims to have founded itself. Senator Edward Robinson even worried that the agency might become an American Gestapo.[12] While that, fortunately, has not happened, much else has. The CIA poses a problem, as Eisenhower acknowledged, calling its activities (specifically, the U2 overflights) "distasteful but vital" and claiming that "we prefer and work for a different kind of world."[13]

Defenses

Defenders of the CIA have responded, in ways that have also become well-rehearsed, to charges that the CIA is both ineffective and un-American.

Specifically, defenders of the agency (1) argue that security policy is subject to substantial oversight by democratically elected officials; (2) claim that security policy is conducted by professionals and, therefore, essentially apolitical so that one need not fret about the abuse of power; and most pervasively, (3) apologize that security policy treats matters of grave danger and radical uncertainty, and therefore failure is unavoidable, and successes (of which there are many) can only be suggested.

The CIA operates under democratic oversight. Defenders of the agency argue that worries about the CIA's abuse of power are groundless, because the agency is subject to oversight by elected officials. The DNI (formerly the DCI) reports regularly to the president. Moreover, the DNI reports to Congress, especially the Senate Select Subcommittee on Intelligence and the House Permanent Select Committee on Intelligence.

The defense is not persuasive, for many reasons. Congress itself feels that oversight is ineffectual and has often said so. From time to time, notably after the Church Report, congressional oversight has been strengthened. But oversight is by definition occasional and after the fact, and therefore driven by known failures.

More generally, insofar as the agency is secret, neither the executive nor the legislative branch has to answer for its performance. Congress does authorize funding for the CIA, but in broad and vague terms, the details of which are known only to a few senior legislators (in negligible danger of losing their seats). As mentioned, the judiciary has rarely, if ever, constrained the CIA. Moreover, the CIA's organic statute allows it to operate outside the law of other countries. While the statute does not go so far, on numerous occasions the CIA has operated outside of international law (which is also the law of the United States, but never mind that) and domestic law, no doubt subordinated to vital national interests. In sum, the CIA operates with a degree of institutional independence enjoyed by no other organ of the U.S. government, not excepting the president. "Oversight" is a fig leaf.

The CIA is professional. Defenders of the CIA claim that, because the CIA is, or at least ideally is, a professional institution, the constitutional criticisms, centering on the abuse of unaccountable power, are inapposite. The CIA is composed of professionals, and because professional life is founded on objective expertise rather than political power, there simply is no reason to worry about the CIA abusing its power.

After 9/11, after the WMD in Iraq fiasco, after the various scandals involving mistreatment, after the agency's lying to the 9/11 Commission, it is impossible to take claims that the CIA is professional, or more bluntly, very good at what it does, seriously. But putting recent unacceptable performance aside for the moment, the agency's claims to professionalism are wrong in principle. To "profess" is to believe, publicly. A secret professional is a contradiction in terms. More subtly, the CIA claims it is professional, that is, objective and independent—it rests its authority on the assertion of expertise. But the conduct of security policy requires the political qualities of subjectivity and connection. We do not need a more expert corps of intelligence agents. We need intelligence officers who understand how the world connects and how to connect to the world.

Uncertainty, danger, and secret successes. Defenders of the CIA frequently argue that the agency does a difficult and dangerous job and therefore has performed well under the circumstances (whatever the circumstances may have been). More specifically, it is frequently said that the dangers facing the United States are both terrible and uncertain. First, terrible: the CIA was founded, in the late '40s, because we did not want "another Pearl Harbor." Almost immediately, we were compelled to worry about a nuclear Pearl Harbor. Talk of the nation's extinction became routine. Now, we have the fear of a nuclear al-Qaeda or similar horror. Second, uncertain: the CIA is charged not with knowledge but with foreknowledge, predicting such attacks and other horrible events so that they may be prevented. But the future is uncertain and hard to predict. Both true. In the face of such danger and uncertainty, this or that failure of the agency is unfortunate but essentially meaningless. All that can be done, in the heroic American tradition, is to get back on the horse; try, try again; and so on.

WHY THE INTELLIGENCE COMMUNITY
HAS NOT YET BEEN REFORMED

After each of its many public failures, the CIA, of course, claims that it should be supported, because (as recent events have demonstrated) the world is a dangerous place. This is almost as predictable as the sun's rising—bureaucracies always justify themselves. And what else are we to do? By definition, a failure by the CIA is a failure of the national security apparatus. The government must act to repair the apparatus, through the CIA or a similar agency. Thus the CIA has almost always already won its argument, even after it has demonstrably failed. That is not to say that the CIA may not, on occasion, be correct. But it is important to remember that while a bureaucracy's self-serving excuses for its shortcomings may be true, they are inherently self-serving. Even if we are helpless to do otherwise, at least as an intellectual matter we should be skeptical about a bureaucracy's claims that it is doing an exemplary, indeed indispensable, job helping the nation to cope with real problems. When, as in security matters, the bureaucracy legitimates itself by playing on our fears, and operates essentially without accountability, we should be intensely skeptical. While completely understandable as a matter of Washington, and national, politics, the position of the CIA—trust us; there are real enemies, and we are doing a very good job of combating them—simply cannot be taken seriously as a matter of institutional thought.

Notwithstanding their failures and structural shortcomings, the CIA and the intelligence institutions have not been reformed. Why not? Bracketing the usual problems with Washington politics, I believe the failure to reform institutions that are so obviously important, and so obviously badly constructed, is largely due to fundamental misconceptions of the nature and purpose of intelligence. From within the box we have constructed for ourselves, there is no way forward. Recall, in the intelligence context, the tautological and apolitical characterization of security policy discussed in Chapter One: (1) intelligence and covert operations are necessary; (2) intelligence and covert operations require unfortunate sacrifices, and horrors can be expected; and (3) the decisions about what is, or is not, to be done are to be left to experts. Thus intelligence escapes actual political thought, much less democratic disputation. Slightly transposed, the same argument makes the scope of the agency's failure unknowable, and its performance therefore beyond assessment; thus intelligence is necessary to protect free societies in a hostile world; intelligence requires moral compromise; intelligence is likely to fail because the world is uncertain, in which case, more intelligence—and more moral compromise—will be necessary.

There are two fatal problems with the orthodox defense of the current structure of our intelligence community, both of which have already been suggested. First, the current structure of the intelligence community is ill-designed to gather real intelligence about the contemporary world, and second, the current structure is profoundly un-American.

THE STRUCTURE OF THE INTELLIGENCE COMMUNITY IS ILL-SUITED TO THE NEW WORLD

We are frequently and truly told that this is a new world, with new kinds of wars. Unsurprisingly, if we consider the traditional intelligence paradigm, we find that it no longer provides a framework for thinking about the world we wish to secure.

1. We do not live in a world of antagonism. There are, of course, conflicts, but none of them, not even that with Osama bin Laden, organizes the world. We have too much to do.
2. The *logic* of fear does not rule. We have fears, of course. But we cannot assume, *a priori*, that others are trying to hurt us and let that assumption guide our political efforts, as we did during the Cold War. More importantly still, we should not give them reason to assume that we are trying to hurt them.
3. Secrecy may be helpful, but it probably is not. Transparency is probably more helpful, in more situations, than secrecy—and, in some cases, requires more courage.
4. Since we are trying to avoid animosity, we cannot treat possible threats as facts. Threats become threats when we are threatened, when we know that somebody wishes to harm us.
5. Since foreign policy, including military affairs and security policy, is subjective and intensely social, devoted to the creation of an order, such enterprises cannot be insulated from politics.
6. The intelligence agencies are deeply political, subjective agents and so, by definition, moral. Intelligence agencies are only secondarily professional, objective experts.

In short, the entire conception of intelligence embodied by the CIA is wrong, that is, wrong for our security situation. This is more than another wasteful bureaucracy. The effort to deny that we are doing politics, and therefore the failure to do politics well, is more than a missed opportunity.

We regularly injure our own prospects. Secrets rarely remain secret, unknown, altogether. The CIA is known to act, or worse, suspected to act, everywhere. Even intelligence gathering, and certainly covert operations, have diplomatic and military, and informal social and political, consequences. The CIA regularly affects our national stature, and thus is doing foreign policy. But because it is a secret agency, the CIA denies responsibility for its actions. *The CIA is the bureaucratic antithesis of the ethos of responsibility that this book has argued ought to inform the exercise of U.S. power.*

As it operates today, the agency presents what in corporation law, and economics generally, is called an "agency problem": The agent (the CIA) is supposed to operate for the benefit of the principal (the U.S. government, and so, we pray, the American people). But the agent operates in an environment without effective controls and often acts in its own interests. Sooner or later, the agent gets the principal in trouble. To make a simple, but I think sound, analogy, the CIA is essentially a wayward, and more than a little self-interested, employee, writing checks for the rest of the government and, by extension, the American people, to cash. This need not be entirely bad hearted. But because it does not do diplomacy and certainly does not do wars, the CIA cannot be expected even to understand the political consequences of its actions. The irresponsible are rarely wise, even when they wish to serve.

These are failures of institutional design.[14]

THE STRUCTURE OF THE U.S. INTELLIGENCE COMMUNITY IS UN-AMERICAN

Eisenhower understated how foreign the CIA is to the American political tradition. Americans have traditionally believed that concentrations of power are dangerous and must be treated with caution. Power tends to defend itself and propagate itself. Power tends to be abused. And power tends to become corrupt, not just in the ordinary sense, but in the more subtle sense of becoming self-absorbed, self-referential, and so ignorant of the world. Concentrations of power are more palatable when they express a democratic will, but even in the case of democracy, presumptively legitimate, Americans have never forgotten Toqueville's lesson that majorities, too, can be tyrannical.

In consequence, a predominant concern of American political thought has been to use law to limit concentrations of power. This is familiar. Our Constitution establishes a federal system, dispersing power between the national government and among the states, and a system of checks and balances so that the various branches of the federal government will constrain possible excesses. And we rely on regular elections to ensure that government does its job well.

These concerns are not confined to the Constitution's ordering of our government. Elsewhere in society, we rely on regulation to bound the activities of the marketplace, and we rely on competition to ensure that people do their jobs well. In both government and the marketplace, we rely on information, transparency, to hold actors accountable. Consider, in this regard, Freedom of Information Act requests, mandatory disclosure under the securities laws, and the importance of the First Amendment rights to freedom of speech and of the press. And we rely on a powerful and independent judiciary system, so that government and nongovernment actors can be made to answer for harms they have caused.

Bureaucratic agencies present special problems for our efforts to prevent the abuse of power. Much bureaucratic work is detailed and technical, done by unelected officials, and somewhat hidden from the restraints recalled by the preceding paragraphs. But government—meaning the tripartite structure of legislative, executive, and judicial branches—retains power over most bureaucracies in numerous ways. Most notably, the funding of agencies is controlled by political processes. The leaders of most agencies serve at the pleasure of the administration, or at least are appointed through bipartisan processes. The judiciary retains extensive rights of review over agency action. Thus, in all sorts of ways, the "headless fourth branch" of the government is, by and large, integrated into the other three, politically limited, branches, and therefore constrained.

The CIA escapes such constraints, and therefore exemplifies and magnifies the constitutional problems posed by bureaucratic power. Not just the details of what the institution does but the details of the institution itself, for example, its budget and the number of its employees, is secret, and not only from the American public but from most of the government. Only the most senior levels of the agency are known, much less subject to an appointment process. The CIA is not restrained by courts; it has a culture of plausible denial. And its work is secret, although we are reassured that successes outnumber failures. The agency is, in a word, unaccountable.

REINTEGRATING INTELLIGENCE INTO STATECRAFT AND WARCRAFT

In the contemporary environment, the question "what is an intelligence asset?" is difficult. Answering the question depends on a rather open-ended, fluid inquiry into what is to be done to secure ourselves in this world. Obviously, gesturing in the direction of the Soviet Union or, for that matter, "Islam" no longer makes sense. We simply cannot presume our enemies, for example, "the terrorists," and then conduct security accordingly. This is not because we have no enemies—as al-Qaeda has demonstrated—but because such enemies need to be fought on political terrain, as our failure to anticipate or even, almost ten years after 9/11, finally defeat al-Qaeda has also demonstrated and as this book has argued. In the present environment, the security question must be, intelligence for what project that increases national, indeed global, security how?

If we need to go so far to ask what counts as intelligence, then it makes no sense to understand intelligence as an enterprise distinct from the conduct of foreign and military affairs broadly construed. The intelligence function should be returned to its tradition, as an indispensable *part* of conducting diplomatic politics (institutionally, in the scheme put forward in this book, as part of the Department of Foreign Affairs) and of the conduct of military politics (under the aegis of the Department of Military Operations).

Placing the conduct of intelligence under the auspices of accountable agencies of government would address most of the structural weaknesses of the current regime. Most obviously, the maintenance and management of spies would be limited by the familiar mechanisms of politics, because the agencies that employed spies, the Departments of Foreign Affairs and Military Operations, would be limited by the executive, legislative, and judicial branches, and more systematically, by the power of transparency and hence responsibility. There would still be secrets (both the State Department and the Department of Defense now have secrets), but secrets would not be the *purpose* of any institution. Secrets might be means to ends, but the ends of responsible, and broadly accountable, institutions.[15]

More subtly, intelligence assets, as redefined within responsible bureaucracies, would have to compete with other bureaucratic priorities. If the Department of Foreign Affairs wants to buy espionage rather than employ a trade expert, we may hope that the choice will be thought through and related to the overarching mission of the institution, for which the Department of Foreign Affairs and ultimately the president will be judged, that is, was foreign policy well practiced? Under the current regime, the State Department will always ask for a diplomat (on the budget), and the CIA will always ask for a spy (off the budget). The chance that Congress will balance these requirements (vis-à-vis a bridge someplace or some other priority) is negligible. The question, within the bureaucracy, must be, if we are to pursue this national interest, for example, diplomatic relations with Tehran, then what do we need? And somebody needs to be responsible for making such choices and for their consequences.

By the same token, it may well be the case that we need enhanced espionage capability, for instance, to find bin Laden or to determine whether some regime is in fact building weapons of mass destruction. The answers may even determine whether we undertake military action. But such questions are not ends in themselves; they are aspects of national security. The military may decide that it needs more spies, but if it is serious about this, the case must be made not in the abstract but against other military priorities, for example, helicopters, in the context of a budget that is broadly transparent.

To state matters very bluntly: isolating the intelligence function within an independent bureaucracy has made the intelligence agencies literally irresponsible. At some level, failure to know is inevitable, and therefore, institutional failures to be intelligent have been excused, for generations now, notwithstanding "another Pearl Harbor" and mistaken wars. Adding insult to injury, "plausible deniability" elevated irresponsibility to the status of a doctrine. Integrating the intelligence function within the diplomatic and military bureaucracies, however, would make intelligence experts more accountable, not least to their peers, and, because more respectable, more effective. There will always be secrets and hence the need for discretion, but neither the diplomatic nor the security posture of the United States should be institutionally deniable, a word uncomfortably close to "shameful."

While this chapter has argued that using an independent agency such as the CIA to run intelligence and covert operations indicates a fundamental misunderstanding of the task at hand, I would reserve at least two roles for a relatively independent office such as the DNI: (1) collation and presentation of intelligence information to leadership and (2) assessment.

The 9/11 Commission got a lot right. Specifically, a DNI that functions as a clearinghouse, a synthesizer of various thoughts on intelligence, makes considerable sense. In particular, if we reintegrate intelligence into the various foreign policy enterprises in which the government is engaged, then it will be necessary to pull together issues and perspectives for policy discourse and for making decisions about what needs further investigation or other action. In much the same vein, it probably makes sense for one official to be primarily responsible for daily briefing of the president, and perhaps relevant members of the National Security Council (NSC), on an all-source basis.

Second, as in other areas of government, there is much to be said for independent assessment. In the first Gulf War, the CIA proved itself better at battlefield damage assessment than the military.[16] The military had no small interest in tabulating its own success; who would not want their attacks to be successful? More generally, intelligence and other security matters could benefit from relatively objective, that is, independent, assessment. So one role for the DNI is as accountant for and evaluator of the intelligence activities of other agencies.

PRELIMINARY RESPONSES TO OBVIOUS OBJECTIONS

This argument will be attacked as hopelessly idealist. But one may be an idealist and still acknowledge that the nation has interests, and that it will act to secure such interests, diplomatically if possible, militarily if need be. Securing those interests costs money, for which we, as a people, pay taxes and forego other goods. Much more importantly, as citizens of a democratic republic, we are held responsible for the politics done in our name. So, in broad outline, we should understand what our government is doing. Democracy requires at least so much. In this republic, even after the change in administration, too much is too secret. Such secrecy is both counterproductive and unworthy. Senators Moynihan and Wyden had it right: "And as we enter the twenty-first century, the great fear we have for our democracy is the enveloping culture of government secrecy and the corresponding distrust of government that follows."[17] A tough-minded idealism is anything but hopeless; we can do better than this.

It also will be argued, with varying degrees of sophistication, that abolishing the CIA would cause the recurrence of the problem that the agency was founded to eliminate: intelligence would not be shared among agencies, and therefore the policy of the United States would be hampered by the low quality of its operational information. Putting to one side the facts that the National Security Act of 1947 did not achieve its goal of integrating intelligence information, and that the Intelligence Reform and Terrorism Prevention Act of 2004 does not look to be a great success, the argument that we need independent intelligence institutions because otherwise intelligence will not be integrated is unpersuasive.

First, as noted above, there is a role for the DNI in coordinating, and in that sense integrating, all source information. The argument here is that we have no need for a CIA, even a restructured one.

Second, and more subtly, I have argued for a political integration of the force projection of the United States, which should encourage the integration of information across organizations. The Department of Foreign Affairs and the Department of Military Operations are different organizations, for the conduct of different aspects of one enterprise, foreign policy. This was Clausewitz's point, with which this book began. We need different organizations, because talking and fighting are very different activities, and because history and tradition matter. But both the diplomatic and military organs of the republic need to know that they are jointly responsible—accountable—for the profound conception and successful execution of the foreign policy of the United States. Because we are trying to construct a security order that requires the participation of others, an order that is globally political even as it seeks to establish national security, we cannot afford to divorce "the military" from "the political." Diplomacy and military operations are part of a continuum, linked by responsibility, and in some deep sense, failure.

To engage in a war represents a failure not only of diplomacy but of government strategy. Because force is often most effective when threatened or used in small amounts and timely fashion, under the institutional structure proposed here, the diplomatic community can be expected to become more hawkish, that is, to keep their military counterparts in the loop. Thus it is in the interest of the Department of Foreign Affairs to involve the Department of Military Operations early, to forestall war or at least limit its intensity or extent.

By the same token, the Department of Military Operations should wish to avoid wars for the simple reason, but worth repeating, that war is bad. Far better a negotiated peace, with peacekeeping troops, than chaos into geno-cide into war into occupation. Conversely, military operations can be suc-cessful only once a durable peace has been established—the military is dependent on the political. And for that reason, military intelligence can be expected to keep their "political" counterparts in the loop, because the moral purpose, and the ultimate success, of military operations is dependent on the reestablishment of political community. More formally, keeping the civilian experts of the Department of Foreign Affairs involved is in the institutional interest of the Department of Military Operations. To great extent, this is happening already—the State Department and the armed services worked very closely together in Iraq and Afghanistan. There is no reason, in princi-ple, that the intelligence services of the two great agencies envisioned here could not similarly work together.

CONCLUSION: FEWER SECRETS, MORE RESPECT

This book has argued that Clausewitz did not follow his insight that war is a form of political expression nearly far enough. *On War* was never finished. War is not merely the expression of the will of the sovereign. War signifies in the world, even among our enemies, and such signification cannot but be political. The strategic idea that we must win the peace, as well as the op-erational and tactical practice of counterinsurgency, all teach that military force is a way of creating social order, and so doing politics, and is therefore a form of foreign policy. The question thus confronts us: how do we Amer-icans, who wage war so often and generally well, wish to do politics? What kind of politics do we want to see established, not just among ourselves, but in the new global order that we have worked so hard to create?

I think the answer to this question is straightforward: we want a world in which people participate in their governance. We want people to be cit-izens. The enterprise of citizenship requires a society that respects the law, and where the truth is available, so that citizens may take responsibility. The United States has undermined its very real desire to see such societies flour-ish by establishing government institutions devoted to the conduct of for-eign policy in secret, and outside the law.

PART FIVE
CONCLUSION

Nor is it any longer possible for you to give up this empire, though there may be some people who in a mood of sudden panic and in a spirit of political apathy actually think this would be a fine and noble thing to do. Your empire is now like a tyranny: it may have been wrong to take it; it is certainly dangerous to let it go.[1]

CHAPTER SEVENTEEN

AGAINST THUCYDIDES

As nations and as individuals, especially in the fullness of our power, we extend ourselves, make commitments. At some point, perhaps, we lead ourselves into temptation, go out too far and find ourselves exposed. What had seemed strength may then come to seem weakness. This is the stuff of tragedy. And as in tragedies in theaters, it is rarely obvious, at the time, that our enthusiasms are veering into transgressions, though perhaps one should treat military invasions (the Athenians in Sicily, the Americans in Iraq) with special caution.

For his part, Thucydides thought that only with great political leadership, an implausible combination of being wise and loved, could Athens navigate the dangers of its own extension. After Pericles died, such leadership was unavailable to the Athenians. Democratic argument failed in typical ways, and the Peloponnesian War was lost. If individual leadership of Periclean caliber is required (which I doubt), the outlook for the United States is no brighter than it was for Athens. The only president who, it might be claimed, was even remotely so wise and loved, Washington, was not produced by the constitutional process. Lincoln was assassinated; Jefferson and Roosevelt were reviled. For all its virtues, the Constitution simply does not ensure that "in what [is] nominally a democracy, power [is] really in the hands of the first citizen."[2]

Still, one should avoid being overly dramatic. Athens had much to contribute after losing the Peloponnesian War. Nations before us have lost preeminence, many gracefully. Besides, I doubt we are at the brink of losing much; I think it is too soon to declare the end of the American century. Certainly no other nation, or postnational form of association, stands ready to fill many of the cultural, economic, and indeed military leadership roles now played by the United States, even though the future no doubt holds its surprises. But to some extent, we must let the future take care of its own. Right now, we citizens of the United States should ask ourselves how our government is to exercise its power, because it is our government, and we are responsible for any transgressions it may commit in our names. And in confronting that issue, we cannot ignore the fact that the United States is vastly and profoundly extended. We have taken positions, globally, from which no easy withdrawal is possible. National power is hardly freedom of action. The United States is very strong but also profoundly constrained by its situation. And in that context, what do we ask when we demand the responsible exercise of our power?

Although the United States is extended and hence constrained, and Athens should be deeply disturbing, our security situation in practice and especially potentially has much to recommend it. We do not face the militarily institutionalized nationalism of the twentieth century, at least not among the truly developed countries. (Whether some of the developing countries, including some very large states, will succeed in modernizing politically without another violent convulsion remains to be seen and is a cause for deep concern.) For all of our worries about weapons of mass destruction, the possibility of annihilation seems much more remote than it did just a generation ago. Starting in Europe, the geographic core of the modernist nightmare, we have learned how to integrate economies and to fragment and synthesize social life in ways that make old-fashioned war almost unimaginable. This is an enormous achievement, this globalization, and with proper management and great good fortune, we may do even more and achieve lasting peace.

But the City of Gold is not yet global; globalization has edges. Germany and France no longer imagine a war, but we still have wars, many of them national or even tribal, some of them all too contemporary. A disconcerting number of these wars are waged in Islamic terms, and fought in, from, or even across, the Muslim world. Precisely because it is constructed to make large-scale violence institutionally and socially and so psychologically difficult if not impossible, the City of Gold has great difficulty responding to such wars.

Security policy, therefore, remains the province of nation-states, and particularly the United States, which often acts unilaterally, superficially, as if this were the nineteenth century, when states understood the right to go to war as part and parcel of their sovereignty and trivially instrumental wars were the order of the day. But this is not the nineteenth, nor even the twentieth, century. Since the Marshall Plan, the purpose of U.S. wars has been to integrate nations into the global order, making repetition of such wars, in such places, highly unlikely. The United States is thus in a profoundly contradictory position. On the one hand, we fight wars in an old-fashioned, rather nationalistic way. On the other hand, insofar as our wars are successful, there will be less cause, and far fewer mechanisms, for such collective violence.

The United States has neither the will nor the means to impose a security order unilaterally. Force alone has its uses but cannot sustain a security order or any form of political life. Politics—and power, the capacity to accomplish things politically—require participation. Specifically, peace can be preserved only if others, even those who might be Islamist radicals, believe that, all things considered, the status quo is worth sustaining. Of course, the existence of opposing force is one of those things that must be considered; I have not here made a pacifist argument. But nonetheless, without subjective belief, the peace will fail.

So the United States finds itself encouraging allegiance to the current security order, that is, making explicit and promoting an ideal of peace embodied by the geopolitical status quo. The United States and, indeed, all peace-loving nations have what may appear to be a difficult case to make. First, the current geopolitical arrangement has, in large part, been achieved through historical injustice; consider the extent to which the map of the world is the product of colonial whimsy or worse. Second, the United States has constructed much of the security order in its own self-interest. Those things said, the status quo is hardly amenable to change—consider the tenacity with which even whimsical borders are maintained. The maintenance of peace, in the sense of nonviolent order, requires making peace, in the sense of accepting, much of the status quo. We must love the world even as it is.

This peace that we citizens of the world have inherited, with all of history's ugliness, is worth having, and even—oh irony of ironies—worth fighting for. Indeed and in broad outline, the United States has no real choice but to fight for some version of the current security order. We have our fears, and there are risks we cannot afford to take. That is what it means to be committed to our own extension. And I believe most people understand that critically important geopolitical, and human, truth.

But appreciating the sadness of history and even sympathizing with the predicaments of U.S. power are far cries from supporting the security order that the United States has tried to establish since the end of the Second World War. To win active support for the order, and thus to ensure our security and, indeed, to justify our use of force, the United States should in some ways withdraw and in other ways become far more present in its dealings abroad.

The United States should withdraw from its exclusive claims to represent the modern, including the modern way of securing peace. We wish others to participate in a security order, that is, to make it their own, too. World peace only works if the people of the world partake in, which practically means to help build, the security order. Presidents Wilson and Roosevelt were right, even if their dreams have proven more difficult to realize than we might have hoped. But the people of the world cannot make the security order their own if "security" is understood to be the exclusive property of the United States. Consequently, the United States should make it clear that we understand that security, indeed peace, is something that we can only achieve together. And in helping to build the security order, citizens from all over the world will make that order less exclusively American, even if it was American in intention and design and even if, for some time hence, we remain the hyperpower, with unequaled capacity for violence. There are many ways for all of us to discover how to be modern while living among one another.

At the same time, the United States should become far more present in its construction of global peace. People cannot do politics with ghosts and phantoms and drones high in the air. We Americans should present ourselves, our government should present itself, more forthrightly. We should be responsible, even if all too human. Quite a lot of politics is possible on the basis of a shared understanding of humanity: certainly peace and perhaps even happiness.

NOTES

EPIGRAPH

1. Ulysses Simpson Grant, *Personal Memoirs of U.S. Grant*, at 17.

CHAPTER ONE: LOOKING OUTWARD

1. Carl von Clausewitz, *On War* 86–87 (J. J. Graham trans., N. Trubner & Co., 1873) (emphasis in original). The *locus classicus* is Clausewitz. *Id.* at bk. 8, ch. 6, 605 et seq.

2. *See* U.S. Const. art. I, § 8 (giving Congress power to declare war); U.S. Const. art. II, § 2 (making president commander-in-chief); *see also* National Defense Act of 1947, Pub. L. No. 80-235, 61 Stat. 496 (1947) (defining the Secretary of Defense as a civilian). The proposition runs throughout U.S. military culture and is perhaps too far beyond debate, in light of the fact that the military is politically engaged in all sorts of ways. *See* A. J. Bacevich, "The Paradox of Professionalism: Eisenhower, Ridgway, and the Challenge to Civilian Control, 1953–1955," 61 *J. Mil. Hist.* 303–33 (1997).

3. If Napoleon announces one of the hallmarks of modernity—mass politics, culture, and military mobilization—then Clausewitz proposes a thoroughly modern response, professional bureaucratization in the service of a politics. Indeed, his famous statement about war as a form of politics was offered, in part, as an excuse: because it was essentially political, thinking about war could not be reduced to its own principles. "[B]ut it is apt to be assumed that war suspends

that [political] intercourse and replaces it by a wholly different condition, ruled by no law but its own. We maintain, on the contrary, that war is simply a continuation of political intercourse, with the addition of other means." Clausewitz, *supra* note 1, at 605. Warfare is not autonomous and thus could not, in the end, be reduced to principles, a law of its own. Therefore, as an intellectual matter, military science could not constitute a discipline in the rigorous way with which Clausewitz, sounding like Kant, began his enterprise. As a political process, bureaucratization (notably the General Staff), understood as rationalization, was inherently dependent, and so limited. There are good reasons that *On War* was never finished and good reasons to consider Clausewitz one of the earliest, and deepest, students of the modern condition.

4. Shades of Arendt's *Eichmann in Jerusalem*.

5. An idea made familiar by the recent renewal of interest in the Nazi theorist Carl Schmitt.

6. *See* Sun-Tzu, *The Art of War: Sun Zi's Military Methods* 129–30 (Victor H. Mair trans, Columbia University Press, 2007) (the state that survives the longest lives frugally and thereby avoids wars); *see also Id.* at 79 (stating the now-famous line, "So to win a hundred victories in a hundred battles is not the highest excellence; the highest excellence is to subdue the enemy's army without fighting at all").

7. *See supra* text accompanying note 1. There are many other ways of understanding war, of course. Consider *The Song of Roland*, or Olivier Roy's *Afghanistan: From Holy War to Civil War*. But the present book assumes the possibility of rational politics, even when the political question is war.

8. It sounds Orwellian, but H. G. Wells wrote *The War that Will End War*. *See* U.S. Army and Marine Corps, *The Army/Marine Corps Counterinsurgency Field Manual* (2007); U.S. Department of Defense, Department of Defense Directive 3000: Policy for Non-Lethal Weapons (July 9, 1996).

9. President Franklin D. Roosevelt, "Fireside Chat: On the Declaration of War with Japan" (Dec. 9, 1941) ("We are going to win the war, and we are going to win the peace that follows.") (transcript available at http://docs.fdrlibrary.marist.edu/120941.html).

10. *See* Clausewitz, *supra* note 1, at 87.

11. This may not always be the case, of course, as demonstrated by recent, and not so recent, history. Grant bitterly noted, "We were sent to provoke a fight, but it was essential that Mexico should commence it. It is very doubtful whether Congress would declare war; but if Mexico should attack our troops, the Executive could announce, . . . whereas, war exists by the acts of, etc., and prosecute the contest with vigor. Once initiated there were but few public men who would

have the courage to oppose it." Ulysses S. Grant, *Grant: Memoirs and Selected Letters* 21 (John Y. Simon ed., 1990). But we commonly understand wars that are not the will of the people as failures of the political process.

12. My thinking here owes a great deal to Olivier Roy. *See* Olivier Roy, *Afghanistan: From Holy War to Civil War* (1995).

13. My usage is in line with that of, and owes debts to, Giles Keppel. *See* Giles Kepel, *Jihad: The Trail of Political Islam* (4th ed., 2003); Giles Kepel, *The War for Muslim Minds: Islam and the West* (Pascale Ghazzaleh trans., 2004).

14. As this book goes to press, "War on Terror" remains current usage in Pakistan, as is "targeted killing" to mean any form of discriminate political violence.

15. This usage has been widely credited to then CENTCOM commander General John Abizaid and picked up by the *2006 Quadrennial Defense Review*. See *Washington Post*, February 3, 2006; *see also* U.S. Department of Defense, *2006 Quadrennial Defense Review* (2006), http://www.defenselink.mil/qdr/archive/20060206qdr1.html (last accessed Nov. 8, 2009). For the use of "Long War" to describe many of the major conflicts of the twentieth century *in toto*, *see* Philip Bobbitt, *The Shield of Achilles: War, Peace and the Course of History* (2003).

16. From an operational perspective, a "Long War" differs substantially from a "Cold War." My understanding is that General Abizaid was trying to lengthen time horizons and politicize conflict, and so to shift the military's thinking from its more objective Cold War and especially Desert Storm (short, sharp conflict with overwhelming force) patterns. But the phrase was used publicly; it was used in the Department of Defense *Quadrennial Review*; it was used by the president. Moreover, "Long War" takes place across great spans of time and space, internationally, like the Cold War, that is, it organizes geographically discrete conflicts. And the ship whose course is being changed, the military, was built during the Cold War—even in change, the past has to be acknowledged. And, most importantly, the phrase "Long War" was and to some extent still is offered as a strategic frame through which the nation can think about how to structure and pay for the military. Thus "Long War" and "Cold War" serve much the same discursive function in security policy. And so the question arises: is the thinking too wedded to Cold War patterns?

CHAPTER TWO: LOOKING INWARD

1. Dwight David Eisenhower, *Public Papers of the Presidents of the United States, Dwight D. Eisenhower, 1960-61* at 1035–1040 (1999) (farewell address on Jan. 17, 1961).

2. *Deuteronomy* 5:18.

3. For a fine overview of contemporary interest in Niebuhr among the chattering class, *see* Paul Elie, "A Man for All Reasons," 300 *The Atlantic* 82 (2007). Niebuhr always denied he was a theologian, maybe because his brother Helmut Richard was a professor of theology. *See id.* at 86.

4. In 1873, Chief Joseph and war chieftains led a band of Nez Perce, including women and children, in a tactically brilliant retreat from the U.S. cavalry that stretched over three months and almost 2,000 miles. Many died. In cold mountains, without food or blankets, the band surrendered, not far from the Canadian border. The Nez Perce were sent to a succession of reservations. The *Iliad* opens, "Sing, goddess, the anger of Peleus' son Achilleus and its devastation, which put pains thousandfold upon the Achaians. . . ." Homer, the *Illiad* bk. 1, ll. 1–3 (Richard Latimore trans, Chicago University Press, 1951). For all the accomplishments of military science, rage continues to play a role. And if any of this book is right, that war is an expression of meaning, and hence always also beyond the bounds of technocracy, then we should continue to reckon on desperation and rage, so far as such reckoning is possible.

5. Gen. Tommy Franks & Malcolm McConnell, *American Soldier* 607 (2005).

CHAPTER THREE: OVERVIEW OF THE ARGUMENT

1. "The doctrine of preemption—the idea that the United States or any other nation can legitimately attack a nation that is not imminently threatening but may be threatening in the future—is a radical new twist on the idea of self-defense." Senator Robert Byrd, "Senate Remarks: We Stand Passively Mute" (Feb. 12, 2003).

2. *See* Ronald Brownstein, *The Second Civil War: How Extreme Partisanship Has Paralyzed Washington and Polarized America* (2007).

3. The satire was of Shona Alexander and James Kilpatrick, who aired an argumentative segment entitled "Point/Counterpoint," on the venerable news program *60 Minutes.*

4. When told that there were legal issues with bombing Kosovo, then secretary of state Madeleine Albright famously said, "Get new lawyers." James P. Rubin, "Countdown to a Very Personal War," *The Fin. Times*, Sept. 30–Oct. 1, 2000, at ix.

5. This point has long been insisted on by Realist scholars of international relations, and generally been denied by international law scholars. Relatively recently, Michael Glennon has forcefully argued as an international lawyer that international law does not govern security questions—an argument I do not

engage here. As the next paragraph suggests, there is much more to say, but this book at least does not attempt to found our thinking about U.S. security policy on an interpretation of the UN Charter, the U.S. Constitution, or other positive law, as important as such laws may be.

6. "[T]hen judging, the by-product of the liberating effect of thinking, realizes thinking, makes it manifest in the world of appearances, where I am never alone and always much too busy to be able to think. The manifestation of the wind of thought is no knowledge; it is the ability to tell right from wrong, beautiful from ugly. And this indeed may prevent catastrophes, at least for myself, in the rare moments when the chips are down." Hannah Arendt, "Thinking and Moral Considerations: A Lecture," 38 *Soc. Res.* 446 (1971).

CHAPTER FOUR: NAMING THE ENEMY

1. "Once it has been determined, from the political conditions, what a war is meant to achieve and what it can achieve, it is easy to chart the course. But great strength of character, as well as great lucidity and firmness of mind, is required in order to follow through steadily, to carry out the plan, and not to be thrown off course by thousands of distractions." Clausewitz, *supra* note 1, at 178.

2. Legal Consequences of the Construction of a Wall in the Occupied Palestinian Territory, Advisory Opinion, *I. C. J. Reports 2004*, p. 136, at para 139.

Judge Higgins conceded that, although Article 51 was not by its terms limited to armed attacks by states, limiting the right to self-defense to states was a fair reading of the ICJ's jurisprudence after military and paramilitary activities in and against Nicaragua *(Nicaragua v. United States of America)* (Merits, Judgment, *I. C. J. Reports 1986*, p. 14). Separate Opinion of Judge Higgins, Para 33.

3. A third conceptual category, that of the pirate, is theoretically available if rather marginal in various ways, but nonetheless of considerable interest. Gerry Simpson, *Law, War and Crime* (2007).

4. *See, e.g.*, Jonathan Freedland, "How London Carried On," *The Guardian*, July 7, 2006, http://www.guardian.co.uk/uk/2006/jul/07/july7.uksecurity4.

5. *See The Torture Papers: The Road to Abu Ghraib* (Karen J. Greenberg & Joshua L. Dratel eds., 2005).

6. David Hume, *A Treatise of Human Nature Being an Attempt to Introduce the Experimental Method of Reasoning Into Moral Subjects and Dialogues Concerning Natural Religion* 195, vol. 2 (1874).

7. This idea that conversation offers intellectual possibilities that are sorely needed at the present time is the theme of my *Navigators of the Contemporary: Why Ethnography Matters.*

CHAPTER FIVE: POLITICAL SUBJECTS

1. There is more than an echo of political liberalism in this image of participating in conversation. Perhaps in contrast to liberal thinkers like Habermas,
Rawls, and my teacher Frank Michelman, however, I do not here require that
the participants in this conversation have much autonomy, at least most of the
time. We are still talking about war, not democracy. But even the vanquished
make meanings, and such meanings may become important to future events—
that is why winning the peace is so important.

2. With apologies to Flaubert.

3. I am, with effort, passing up this opportunity to make jokes about Bill
Clinton.

CHAPTER SIX: POLITICS IS NOW

1. *See* Bernard Lewis, *What Went Wrong?: Western Impact and Middle Eastern
Response* (2002).

2. A point demonstrated in the work of Amel Boubekeur.

3. John M. Broder, "For Muslim Who Says Violence Destroys Islam,
Violent Threats," *New York Times*, Mar. 11, 2006, http://www.nytimes.com/
2006/03/11/international/middleeast/11sultan.html.

4. "Certainly the unhesitating and unreasoning way in which we feel we
must inflict our Civilization upon 'lower' races, by means of Hotchkiss guns,
etc., reminds one of nothing so much as of the early spirit of Islam spreading
its religion by the sword." William James, *The Varieties of Religious Experience*,
at 69.

5. An Nai'im has done just that.

6. The echo of Marx's, "On the Jewish Question," and more generally, the
failure of nineteenth- and twentieth-century Europe to answer the question in
humane fashion, is intended.

7. *See generally* Olivier Roy, *Globalized Islam* (2004).

8. Oxford English Dictionary; Thucydides, *The History of the Peloponnesian
War 47* (M. I. Finley ed., Rex Warner trans., 1954) (discussing differences in
scale between modern and ancient warfare).

9. *See generally* David A. Westbrook, "Theorizing the Diffusion of Law:
Conceptual Difficulties, Unstable Imaginations, and the Effort To Think
Gracefully Nonetheless," Keynote Address Before the International Law Journal
Symposium: The Diffusion of Law in the 21st Century (Mar. 4, 2006), 47
Harv. Int'l L.J., 2006, at 489–506.

10. William Faulkner, *Requiem for a Nun* act II, scene 1 (1975).

CHAPTER SEVEN: THE MODERNISM OF RADICAL NEOFUNDAMENTALISM

1. Such explanations give intellectuals a chance to play our traditional (at least since the Dreyfus Affair) role, and are therefore comforting for people like me.

2. It must be stressed that this is only a sketch. I am an emphatically Western intellectual, even if I have a long-standing interest in matters Islamic. But my topic here is not Islam or even bin Laden's War per se but how such distant concepts may be—indeed inevitably must be—appropriated by policy elites, and made the objects of political dispute, especially in my own nation. Rephrased, foreign policy is inevitably based on misapprehensions, journalism rather than history, but must be undertaken nonetheless.

3. The conceptions were reached sequentially, chronologically, but all are vibrant now. Because later conceptions do not necessarily supersede earlier conceptions, few if any Muslims would think of the tradition as a narrative of evolution or progress.

4. For discussion and bibliography, see Westbrook, David A., "Islamic International Law and Public International Law: Separate Expressions of World Order," 33 *Va. J. Int'l L*. 819 (1993).

5. *See generally* Olivier Roy, *The Failure of Political Islam* (1994).

6. Hannah Arendt, *On Revolution* 57 (1965).

7. "Culture" here must be bracketed, because we are talking about forming community, in modern fashion, without the continuities of time and place understood in traditional societies, and in classical anthropology, to delimit culture.

8. George W. Bush, *The National Security Strategy of the United States of America—September 2002* at 228 (2002).

CHAPTER EIGHT: ALL POLITICS IS SPATIAL

1. Networks have been a common way to describe and understand terrorism. *See, e.g.*, Marc Sageman, *Understanding Terror Networks* (2004); Mariam Abou Zahab & Olivier Roy, *Islamist Networks: The Afghan-Pakistan Connection* (2004).

2. The more geographical, at least after Bismark, "German" would be contrary to Schmitt's thrust.

3. *See* Tip O'Neill & Gary Hymel, *All Politics Is Local and Other Rules of the Game* (1994).

4. See generally Eyal Weizman.

5. In Afghanistan, however, General Tommy Franks said, "We don't do body counts." Edward Epstein, "Success in Afghan War Hard to Gauge: U.S. Reluctance to Produce Body Counts Makes Proving Enemy's Destruction Difficult,"

San Francisco Chron., March 23, 2002, http://www.sfgate.com/cgi-bin/article.cgi ?f=/c/a/2002/03/23/MN218394.DTL.

CHAPTER NINE: BIN LADEN'S CHALLENGE

1. What I am doing here requires the reader's trust. I am articulating a position or a logic, something akin to but less than a philosophy, that arises within a social situation. Such logics may or may not be so clearly articulated by the participants. This frank intervention by the author is troubling to modern historians, although Thucydides regularly does the same thing, from time to time stopping his account of the war to stage a play.

2. Thomas Friedman, "America vs. The Narrative," *New York Times*, November 29, 2009.

3. Many, perhaps most, terrorists organizations make grand theoretical claims, even though they have few practical capabilities. The classic chronological overview is Bruce Hoffman's. *See* Bruce Hoffman, *Inside Terrorism* (2006).

4. The arcadian visions of anarchists, including the Unabomber, and the dictatorship of the proletariat in Marxist thought, similarly *oriented* violence.

5. Sayyid Qutb was an ideologue of political Islam who advocated revolution and who was hanged by the Egyptian government in 1960. *See* Sayyid Qutb, *Milestones* (3rd ed., Markazi Maktaba Islami, 1991).

6. It must be stressed that this is a radical perspective. Many Islamic scholars have condemned every aspect of the arguments sketched here under the banner of bin Laden; what is here ascribed to bin Laden should by no means be taken as definitive Islamic belief. Doctrinal issues are always complicated and are made more so in the Muslim context by the absence of a recognized church, so there is no "official" position—there are many positions, of varying, and highly contested, authority.

7. National Commission on Terrorist Attacks Upon the United States, *The 9/11 Commission Report: Final Report of the National Commission on Terrorist Attacks Upon the United States* sec. 7 (2004).

8. Thomas L. Friedman, "A Poverty of Dignity and a Wealth of Rage," *New York Times*, July 15, 2005, http://www.nytimes.com/2005/07/15/opinion/15 friedman.html.

9. *Paradise Now*, the title of a recent movie about suicide bombing, hardly suggests a negotiating stance. *See Paradise Now* (Warner Bros. 2005).

10. Those who have given up discovering a protostate, and hence political rationality, in al-Qaeda often turn to irrationality. So, it is argued, al-Qaeda expresses the rage of traditional cultures repressed by the forces of modernization,

especially globalization. But the diverse bands of fighters, many of them converts or minorities and most thousands of miles from home, do not fight to defend an indigenous culture against the encroachments of modernity, for the simple reason that they share little culture in the sense of the collective understanding and practices of a people in a particular place. Nor do they share a traditional or developed idea of Islam—many learned their Islam when, not before, they became radicalized. This is not some sort of aboriginal violence that will subside once the natives have been properly assimilated; many of the 9/11 bombers had studied engineering. Global Jihad is a very contemporary, even postmodern, phenomenon. Consequently, while it is to be hoped that Global Jihad will pass into history, there is nothing about the process of modernization that makes this necessary.

11. The Baader-Meinhof Gang terrorized what was then West Germany through the 1970s, resulting in the deaths of scores of people. *See generally* Anthony Glees, *Reinventing Germany: German Political Development since 1945* (1996). On April 19, 1995 Timothy McVeigh bombed the Alfred P. Murrah Federal Building. *See* Geraldine Giordano, *Terrorist Attacks: The Oklahoma City Bombing* (2003).

12. Recall, again, that Clausewitz speaks of the wars of what he calls "civilized people," that is, Clausewitz explicitly assumes what we have come to call a Weberian modernity, in which the rationalistic mechanisms of bureaucratic governments prosecute wars in order to achieve politically determined ends (which is hardly the same thing as saying the wars themselves are rational).

13. To suggest a theological argument that perhaps deserves more work: radical neofundamentalism is a decisive rupture with the Islamic tradition, even at its most militant, because of its relationship to violence. Radical neofundamentalism pays more attention to the enemies of the *ummah* than to the *ummah* itself. In so doing, radical neofundamentalism understands Islam through violence, that is, radical neofundamentalism is so dependent on its enemies that it has given up the possibility of a specifically Islamic affirmation.

14. Thomas Friedman, "America vs. The Narrative," *New York Times*, November 29, 2009.

CHAPTER TEN: IDEOLOGICAL ABSTRACTION AND CONCRETE PRESENCE

1. President George W. Bush, "President's Address to the Nation on the War on Terror in Iraq," 43 *Weekly Comp. of Pres. Doc.* 19–23 (Jan. 10, 2007).

2. Mary Anne Weaver, "Inventing Al-Zarqawi," 297 *The Atlantic Monthly* 87, 100 (July/August 2006).

3. "In an insurgency, the way to destroy the insurgent is to attack him at the source of his strength: the population." Andrew F. Krepinevich, *The Army and Vietnam* 10 (1986).

4. Mao Tse-Tung, *On Guerrilla Warfare* (Samuel B. Griffith II trans., 1961).

5. For similarly vast numbers, see Michael J. Watts, "Revolutionary Islam: A Geography of Modern Terror," in *Violent Geographies: Fear, Terror, and Political Violence* 175–204 (Allan Pred and Derek Gregory eds., 2007).

CHAPTER ELEVEN: PEACETIME CONTESTS

1. *See* Pierre d'Argent & David A. Westbrook, "Après le 11 septembre, l'Amérique," *3 La Revue Nouvelle* 89–99.

2. On the conceptual confusion between "globalization" and "Americanization," *see* David A. Westbrook's "The Globalization of American Law," *Theory, Culture and Society, Special Issue on Problematizing Global Knowledge* 526–528, vol. 23.

3. The most obvious way of fostering autonomy, of course, is material—can people earn a living? While ensuring employment presents any number of problems, certain barriers to employment can easily and should be lifted, most notably the various barriers to the free flow of agricultural products that the now-stalled Doha round of the trade talks again failed to resolve. The benefit that the poorest countries currently receive as aid from developed countries would be dwarfed by the benefit the poorest countries would receive by being able to compete in global agricultural markets. Therefore, if we are serious about global security, and especially about threats emanating out of poor countries in the Islamic world, we should do all that we can to ensure that agriculture and other local enterprises are possible.

CHAPTER TWELVE: WARTIME CONTESTS

1. Eliot A. Cohen, "History and Hyperpower," *83 Foreign Aff.* 49–63 (2004).

2. *See generally* Lionel Trilling, *The Liberal Imagination* 118 (1978).

3. There seems to be a resurgence of interest in Kipling in the academy.

4. Thucydides gives me pause. "Our opinion of the gods and our knowledge of men lead us to conclude that it is a general and necessary law of nature to rule whatever one can. This is not a law that we made ourselves, nor were we the first to act upon it when it was made. We found it already in existence, and we shall leave it to exist forever among those who come after us." Thucydides, Book V, 105 (the Melian Dialogue) *supra* ch. 6, note 8, 404-05.

5. Andrew J. Bacevich, "I Lost My Son to a War I Oppose. We Were Both Doing Our Duty," *The Wash. Post.*, May 27, 2007, http://www.washingtonpost .com/wp-dyn/content/article/2007/05/25/AR2007052502032.html.

6. Daniele Deane, "D.C. Man Killed in Suicide Attack at Hotel," Jan. 16, 2008, http://www.washingtonpost.com/wp-dyn/content/article/2008/01/15/ AR2008011503301.html.

7. Joseph Conrad, *Heart of Darkness* 9 (Stanley Appelbaum ed., 1990).

8. Rudyard Kipling, "The Ballad of East and West," in *The Collected Poems of Rudyard Kipling* 245–248 (1994).

9. *See* Samuel P. Huntington, *The Clash of Civilizations and the Remaking of World Order* (1998). Huntington's thesis had already enjoyed enormous popularity with Islamic fundamentalists in the 1990s. *Rethinking Civilizational Analysis* 9 (Saïd Amir Arjomand & Edward A. Tiryakian eds., 2004).

CHAPTER THIRTEEN: NEW WORLD SECURITY

1. National Security Act of 1947, Pub. L. No. 80-235, 61 Stat. 496 (provisions effective Sept. 18, 1947).

2. *See also* The Central Intelligence Agency Act of 1949, Pub. L. No. 81-110, 63 Stat. 208 (1949).

3. *See generally* Andrew J. Bacevich, *The New American Militarism: How Americans Are Seduced by War* (2005).

CHAPTER FOURTEEN:
THE DEPARTMENT OF FOREIGN AFFAIRS

1. I understand, and have tried to argue throughout, that security policy is usually pursued in different ways at the same time, and that these different approaches to the nation's security will occupy different points along the continuum of violence. Nonetheless, we may also fairly imagine a given security crisis in narrative fashion.

CHAPTER FIFTEEN:
THE DEPARTMENT OF MILITARY OPERATIONS

1. National Security Act of 1947, Pub. L. No. 80-235, 61 Stat. 496 (provisions effective Sept. 18, 1947).

2. Ronald Reagan, Pres., U.S., Remarks at the Annual Convention of the National Association of Evangelicals in Orlando, Florida (Mar. 8, 1983), http://

reaganfoundation.org/pdf/Remarks_Annual_Convention_National_Association_Evangelicals_030883.pdf.

3. The executive branch already holds both olive branches and arrows. The president is the head of state and the commander in chief, and therefore is responsible for the coherence, or lack thereof, of our foreign policy. Rather more bureaucratically, the National Security Act of 1947, see *supra* text accompanying ch. 1, note 2, established a National Security Council, formally composed of heads of both military and diplomatic agencies and practically involving others believed by the administration to be helpful in formulating policy. Thus, as a matter of presidential counsel, there is a synthesis of amicable and violent politics. But the NSC is the insider's organization par excellence, shadowy and little understood, and despite its statutory establishment, essentially molded by individual presidents. *See generally* David J. Rothkopf, *Running the World* (2004). After decrying various Hollywood mischaracterizations of foreign and military policy making, Rothkopf describes such policy, since the National Security Act of 1947; in literally Shakespearean terms. *See* Rothkopf, *supra* note 95, at 13–14. While no doubt an effort at cleverness and perhaps a certain grandeur, Rothkopf's portrayal of the presidency, and especially its security apparatus, in terms of courtly intrigue is repugnant to his own republican pieties and Enlightened desires. Whether we have the wherewithal to establish a less Byzantine executive apparatus I leave to the reader's consideration—this book has attempted more than enough.

4. "Do political relations between peoples and between their governments stop when diplomatic notes are no longer exchanged? Is war not just another expression of their thoughts, another form of speech or writing? Its grammar, indeed, may be its own, but not its logic." Clausewitz, *supra* ch. 1, note 1, at 605.

5. *See, e.g.,* Grant, *supra* note 14, at 83–89.

6. Goldwater-Nichols Department of Defense Reorganization Act of 1986, Pub. L. No. 99-433, 100 Stat. 994 (1986).

7. *Id.*

8. *See* U.S. Dep't of Army, *Field Manual 3-24.2, Tactics in Counterinsurgency* (Apr. 21, 2009).

9. "We have now ended the 6th day of very hard fighting. The result up to this time is much in our favor. But our losses have been heavy as well as those of the enemy. We have lost at this time eleven general officers killed, wounded and missing, and *probably twenty thousand men*. I think the loss of the enemy must be greater . . . ," U.S. Grant to Maj. Gen. Halleck, Chief of Staff of the Army, May 11th, 1864 (after the battle of Spottsylvania Court House) (emphasis added). Quoted in Grant, *supra* note 14, at 321.

10. *Cf.* Krepinevich, *supra* note 74, at 5 (speaking of the American reliance on high volumes of firepower to minimize casualties—in effect, the substitution of material costs at every available opportunity to avoid payment in blood).

CHAPTER SIXTEEN:
THE REINTEGRATION OF INTELLIGENCE

1. Reinhold Niebuhr, *Moral Man and Immoral Society: A Study in Ethics and Politics* (1934).

2. *See* Sun-Tzu, *supra* ch. 1, note 6, at ch. 13.

3. *See* David Kahn, "The Rise of Intelligence," 85 *Foreign Aff.* 125–135 (2006) (noting at the same that it is force, not intelligence, that wins wars).

4. In short, most intelligence is false, and the effect of fear is to multiply lies and inaccuracies. As a rule, most men would rather believe bad news than good, and rather tend to exaggerate the bad news. *See* Clausewitz, *supra* ch. 1, note 1, at 117.

5. Intelligence Reform and Terrorism Prevention Act of 2004, Pub. L. No. 108-458, 118 Stat. 3638 (2004) (codified at 40 U.S.C. § 401 et seq.).

6. This was more true than the 9/11 Commission realized. It later emerged that the CIA had lied to the 9/11 Commission, presumably in the national, our, interest. *See, e.g.*, Mark Mazzetti, "9/11 Panel Study Finds That C.I.A. Withheld Tapes," *New York Times*, Dec. 22, 2007, http://www.nytimes.com/2007/12/22/washington/22intel.html.

7. It is worth pointing out that most forms of intellectual property, notably patent and copyright, are not secret. They are, instead, protected by open legal processes.

8. Possibly apocryphal, attributed to President Franklin Roosevelt, speaking of Nicaraguan dictator Anastasio Somoza. Whoever said it first, our Cold War politics provided numerous chances to use the line.

9. NSC 10/2, Foreign Relations of the United States, Emergence of the Intelligence Establishment, 1945–1950 (1996), *microformed on* Supplement (U.S. Gov't Printing Office). *See* David M. Barrett, *CIA and Congress: The Untold Story from Truman to Kennedy* 31–32 (2005).

10. David Kahn notes, "[T]he most successful general staff of all [the Prussian] never set up a permanent peacetime agency for the evaluation of intelligence. Intelligence was only permanently institutionalized after Germany's defeat in World War One." Kahn, at 130.

11. *See* Barrett, *supra* note 111, at 323 et seq. (Subordinating Intelligence, especially the exchange between DCI Dulles and Senator Symington).

12. Barrett, *supra* note 111, at 9.

13. "News Conference Statement by the President, May 11, 1960." (Available: http://www.pbs.org/wgbh/amex/presidents/34_eisenhower/psources/ps_u2.html #top)

14. The structure of the CIA is not even good for the intelligence community, if we understand the community professionally, in terms of the experts who make it up, rather than in terms of particular bureaucratic entities. "Independent" may also mean isolated. On a number of occasions, the CIA appears to have been misdirected by its own leadership, by the White House, and even by a member of Congress, into actions against the better judgment of the intelligence analysts. But bound by their need to maintain independence, i.e., secrecy, there was no institutionally countervailing force, and bad policies were executed.

15. Unfortunately, the Department of Defense has grown less accountable in recent years, as the size of the classified budget has been greatly increased.

16. *See* Richard L. Russell, "CIA's Stragetic Intelligence in Iraq," in *September 11, Terrorist Attacks, and U.S. Foreign Policy* 111–128 (Demetrios Caraley ed., 2002). (The CIA was subsequently relieved of responsibility for battlefield damage assessment.)

17. Senators Daniel Patrick Moynihan & Ron Wyden, "Secrecy in International and Domestic Policy Making: The Case for More Sunshine," in *Fed'n of Am. Scientists*, Oct. 2000, http://www.fas.org/sgp/library/wyden.html.

CHAPTER SEVENTEEN: AGAINST THUCYDIDES

1. Pericles, as recounted by Thucydides in *The Peloponnesian War*, Book II. Thucydides, *supra* ch. 6, note 48, at 161.

2. Thucydides, *supra* ch. 6, note 48, at 164.

BIBLIOGRAPHY

Abbas, Hassan. *Pakistan's Drift into Extremism: Allah, the Army, and America's War on Terror.* New York: M.E. Sharpe, Inc., 2004.

Abu-Assad, Hany, and Bero Beyer. *Paradise Now.* DVD. Directed by Hany Abu-Assad. Los Angeles, CA: Warner Bros, 2005.

Allen, Chris, et al. *European Islam: Challenges for Public Policy and Society.* Edited by Samir Amghar, Amel Boubekeur, and Michael Emerson. Brussels: Centre for European Policy Studies, 2007

Anderson, Sean K., and Stephen Sloan. *Historical Dictionary of Terrorism.* 3rd ed. Lanham, MA: Scarecrow Press, 2009.

An-Na'im, Abdullahi Ahmed. *Islam and the Secular State: Negotiating the Future of Shari'a.* Cambridge MA: Harvard University Press, 2010.

———. *Toward an Islamic Reformation: Civil Liberties, Human Rights, and International Law.* Syracuse, NY: Syracuse University Press, 1996.

Arendt, Hannah. *Eichmann in Jerusalem.* London: Penguin Classics, 2006.

———. *On Revolution.* London: Penguin Books, 1965.

———. "Thinking and Moral Considerations: A Lecture." *Social Research,* 1971: 417–446.

Arjomand, Saïd Amir, and Edward A. Tiryakian. *Rethinking Civilizational Analysis.* London: SAGE Publications Ltd., 2004.

Arquilla, John, and David Ronfeldt. *Networks and Netwars: The Future of Terror, Crime, and Militancy.* Santa Monica, CA: RAND, 2001.

Bacevich, A. J. *American Empire: The Realities & Consequences of U.S. Diplomacy.* Cambridge, MA: President and Fellows of Harvard College, 2002.

————. "I Lost My Son to a War I Oppose. We Were Both Doing Our Duty." *The Washington Post,* May 27, 2007. http://www.washingtonpost.com/wp-dyn/content/article/2007/05/25/AR2007052502032.html (accessed November 8, 2009).

————. *The New American Militarism: How Americans Are Seduced by War.* New York: Oxford University Press, 2005.

————. "The Paradox of Professionalism: Eisenhower, Ridgway, and the Challenge to Civilian Control, 1953–1955." *The Journal of Military History* 61, no. 2 (April 1997): 303–333.

————, ed. *The Long War: A New History of U.S. National Security Policy Since World War II.* New York: Columbia University Press, 2007.

Barnett, Thomas P. M. *The Pentagon's New Map: War and Peace in the Twenty-First Century.* New York: G. P. Putnam's Sons, 2004.

Barrett, David M. *CIA and Congress: The Untold Story from Truman to Kennedy.* Lawrence: University of Kansas Press, 2005.

Benjamin, Daniel, and Steven Simon. *The Age of Sacred Terror: Radical Islam's War Against America.* New York: Random House, 2003.

————. *The Next Attack: The Failure of the War on Terror and a Strategy for Getting It Right.* New York: Times Books, 2005.

Bobbitt, Philip. *The Shield of Achilles: War, Peace and the Course of History.* New York: Penguin, 2003.

————. *Terror and Consent: The Wars for the Twenty-First Century.* New York: Random House, 2008.

Boubekeur, Amel. "Political Islam in Algeria." *CEPS Working Documents No. 268.* Centre for European Policy Studies. May 2007. http://www.ceps.eu/ceps/download/1331 (accessed November 1, 2009).

————. "Post-Islamist Culture: A New Form of Mobilization?" *History of Religions* 47, no. 1 (2007): 75–94.

Broder, John M. "For Muslim Who Says Violence Destroys Islam, Violent Threats." *The New York Times,* March 11, 2006. http://www.nytimes.com/2006/03/11/international/middleeast/11sultan.html (accessed November 1, 2009).

Brownstein, Ronald. *The Second Civil War: How Extreme Partisanship Has Paralyzed Washington and Polarized America.* New York: Penguin Group, 2007.

Bush, George W. "Address to the Nation on the War on Terror in Iraq." *Weekly Compilation of Presidential Documents* 43, no. 2 (January 10, 2007). Speech. Washington, DC: National Archives and Records Administration: 19–23.

————. *The National Security Strategy of the United States of America—September 2002.* Washington DC: The White House, 2002.

Byrd, Robert C. "Senate Remarks: We Stand Passively Mute." Speech. Washington, DC, February 12, 2003.

Carr, Matthew. *The Infernal Machine: A History of Terrorism.* New York: New Press, 2007.

Chua, Amy. *Day of Empire: How Hyperpowers Rise to Global Dominance—and Why They Fall.* New York: Doubleday, 2007.

Clarke, Richard A., et al. *Defeating the Jihadists: A Blueprint for Action.* New York: Century Foundation Press, 2005.

Clausewitz, Carl von. *On War.* Translated by J. J. Graham. London: N. Trubner & Co., 1873.

Cohen, Eliot A. "History and Hyperpower." *Foreign Affairs* 83, no. 63 (2004): 49–63.

Coll, Steven. *Ghost Wars: The Secret History of the CIA, Afghanistan, and Bin Laden, from the Soviet Invasion to September 10, 2001.* New York: Penguin Press, 2004.

Conrad, Joseph. *Heart of Darkness.* Edited by Stanley Appelbaum. Mineola, NY: Dover, 1990.

Cooley, John. *Unholy Wars: Afghanistan, America and International Terrorism.* London: Pluto Press, 2002.

Corbin, Jane. *Al Qaeda: In Search of the Terrorist Network that Threatens the World.* New York: Thunder's Mouth Press/Nation Books, 2003.

Crile, George. *Charlie Wilson's War: The Extraordinary Story of the Largest Covert Operation in History.* New York: Grove Press, 2003.

d'Argent, Pierre, and David A. Westbrook. "Après le 11 septembre, l'Amérique." *La Revue Nouvelle* 3 (2003): 89–99.

Darling, Arthur B. *The Central Intelligence Agency: An Instrument of Government to 1950.* University Park: The Pennsylvania State University Press, 1990.

Dawisha, Adeed. *Arab Nationalism in the Twentieth Century: From Triumph to Despair.* Princeton, NJ: Princeton University Press, 2003.

Delong, Lt. Gen. Michael, Noah Lukeman, and Gen. Anthony Zinni. *A General Speaks Out: The Truth About the Wars in Afghanistan and Iraq.* St. Paul, MN: MBI Publishing Co., 2007.

Drogin, Bob. *Curveball: Spies, Lies, and the Con Man Who Caused a War.* New York: Random House, 2007.

Eisenhower, Dwight David. *Public Papers of the Presidents of the United States, Dwight D. Eisenhower, 1960–61.* Washington, DC: United States Government Printing Office, 1999.

Elie, Paul. "A Man for All Reasons." *The Atlantic* 300, no. 4 (November 2007): 82.

Epstein, Edward. "Success in Afghan War Hard to Gauge: U.S. Reluctance to Produce Body Counts Makes Proving Enemy's Destruction Difficult." *San Francisco Chronicle*, March 23, 2002. http://www.sfgate.com/cgi-bin/article.cgi?f=/c/a/2002/03/23/MN218394.DTL (accessed November 8, 2009).

Faulkner, William. *Requiem for a Nun.* New York: Random House, 1975.

Ferguson, Niall. *Empire: The Rise and Demise of the British World Order and the Lessons for Global Power.* New York: Penguin Books, 2002.

Franks, Gen. Tommy, and Malcolm McConnell. *American Soldier.* New York: HarperCollins Publishers, 2004.

Freedland, Jonathan. "How London Carried On." *The Guardian,* July 7, 2006. http://www.guardian.co.uk/uk/2006/jul/07/july7.uksecurity4 (accessed November 8, 2009).

Friedman, Thomas L. "America vs. The Narrative." *The New York Times*, November 29, 2009.

———. "A Poverty of Dignity and a Wealth of Rage." *The New York Times,* July 15, 2005. http://www.nytimes.com/2005/07/15/opinion/15friedman.html (accessed November 1, 2009).

Gaddis, John Lewis. *Surprise, Security, and the American Experience.* Cambridge, MA: President and Fellows of Harvard College, 2004.

Giddens, Anthony, and Christopher Pierson. *Conversations with Anthony Giddens: Making Sense of Modernity.* Stanford, CA: Stanford University Press, 1998.

Giordano, Geraldine. *Terrorist Attacks: The Oklahoma City Bombing.* New York: Rosen Publishing Group, 2003.

Glees, Anthony. *Reinventing Germany: German Political Development since 1945.* Oxford: Berg Publishers, 1996.

Gohari, M. J. *The Taliban: Ascent to Power.* Oxford: Oxford University Press, 1999.

Gourevitch, Philip, and Errol Morris. *Standard Operating Procedure.* London: Penguin Press, 2008.

Grant, Ulysses S. *Grant: Memoirs and Selected Letters.* Edited by John Y. Simon. New York: Literary Classics of the United States, 1990.

Gray, Colin S. *Another Bloody Century: Future Warfare.* London: Phoenix Press, 2006.

Greenberg, Karen J., and Joshua L. Dratel, eds. *The Torture Papers: The Road to Abu Ghraib.* New York: Cambridge University Press, 2005.

Gregory, Derek, and Allan Pred. *Violent Geographies: Fear, Terror, and Political Violence.* New York: Routledge, 2007.

Gunaratna, Rohan. *Inside Al Qaeda: Global Network of Terror.* New York: Columbia University Press, 2002.

Halliday, Fred. *Nation and Religion in the Middle East.* Boulder, CO: Lynne Rienner Publishers, 2000.

Hegghammer, Thomes. "FFI 2002/01393." Vers. Swedish. *Dokoumt asjon om Al-qaida Intervjuer Kommunikeer og Andre Primaerkider, 1990–2002.* 2002. http://rapporter.ffi.no/rapporter/2002/01393.pdf (accessed November 1, 2009).

Hoffman, Bruce. *Inside Terrorism.* New York: Columbia University Press, 2006.

Homer. *The Illiad.* Translated by Richard Latimore. Chicago, IL: Chicago University Press, 1951.

Hume, David. *A Treatise of Human Nature Being an Attempt to Introduce the Experimental Method of Reasoning Into Moral Subjects and Dialogues Concerning Natural Religion.* London: Longmans, Green, and Co., 1874.

Huntington, Samuel P. *The Clash of Civilizations and the Remaking of World Order.* New York: Simon & Schuster, 1998.

———, ed. *The Clash of Civilizations?: The Debate.* New York: Foreign Affairs Books, 1993.

Hussain, Raja G. *Badal: A Culture of Revenge: The Impact of Collateral Damage on Taliban Insurgency.* Master's thesis. Naval Postgraduate School, 2008.

James, William. *The Varieties of Religious Experience: A Study in Human Nature: Being the Gifford Lectures on Natural Religion Delivered at Edinburgh in 1901–1902.* New York: Longmass, Green, and Co., 1905.

Johnson, Loch K. *America's Secret Power: The CIA in a Democratic Society.* New York: Oxford University Press, 1989.

Kahn, David. "The Rise of Intelligence." *Foreign Affairs* 85, no. 5 (2006): 125–135.

Kaplan, Robert D. *Imperial Grunts: The American Military and the Ground.* New York: Random House, 2005.

———. *Warrior Politics: Why Leadership Demands a Pagan Ethos.* New York: Random House, 2002.

Karsh, Efrahim. *Islamic Imperialism: A History.* New Haven, CT: Yale University Press, 2007.

Keegan, John. *Intelligence in War: Knowledge of the Enemy from Napoleon to Al-Quaeda.* New York: Random House, 2003.

Kepel, Gilles. *Jihad: The Trail of Political Islam.* 4th ed. London: I.B. Tauris & Co. Ltd., 2003.

———. *The War for Muslim Minds: Islam and the West.* Translated by Pascale Ghazzaleh. Cambridge, MA: Harvard University Press, 2004.

Kessler, Ronald. *Inside the CIA.* New York: Pocket Books, 1992.

Kipling, Rudyard. *The Collected Poems of Rudyard Kipling.* Ware, Hertfordshire: Wordsworth, 1994.

Kissinger, Henry. *Diplomacy.* New York: Simon & Schuster, 1994.

———. *Does America Need a Foreign Policy?: Toward a Diplomacy for the 21st Century.* New York: Simon & Schuster, 2001.

Krepinevich, Andrew F. *The Army and Vietnam.* Baltimore, MD: The Johns Hopkins University Press, 1986.

Kristol, William. "Democrats Should Read Kipling." *The New York Times,* February 18, 2008. http://www.nytimes.com/2008/02/18/opinion/18 kristol.html (accessed November 1, 2009).

Küentzel, Mattias. *Jihad and Jew-Hatred: Islamism, Nazism and the Roots of 9/11.* New York: Telos Press Publishing, 2007.

Laqueur, Walter. *The Age of Terrorism.* Boston, MA: Little & Brown, 1987.

———. *A History of Terrorism.* New Brunswick, NJ: Transaction Publishers, 2001.

———. *The New Terrorism: Fanaticism and the Arms of Mass Destruction.* Oxford: Oxford University Press, 1999.

———. *No End to War: Terrorism in the 21st Century.* New York: Continuum Publishing Group, 2003.

———, ed. *Voices of Terror: Manifestos, Writings and Manuals of Al Qaeda, Hamas, and Other Terrorists from Around the World and Throughout the Ages.* Naperville, IL: Reed Press, 2004.

Lennon, Alexander T. J., ed. *The Battle for Hearts and Minds: Using Soft Power to Undermine Terrorist Networks.* Cambridge, MA: The MIT Press, 2003.

Lesser, Ian O., Bruce Hoffman, John Arquilla, David Rondfeldt, and Michele Zanini. *Countering the New Terrorism.* Santa Monica, CA: RAND, 1999.

Lewis, Bernard. *From Babel to Dragomans: Interpreting the Middle East.* Oxford: Oxford University Press, 2004.

———. *Race and Slavery in the Middle East: An Historical Enquiry.* Oxford: Oxford University Press, 1990.

———. "The Roots of Muslim Rage." *The Atlantic Monthly* 266, no. 3 (September 1990): 47–60.

———. *What Went Wrong?: Western Impact and Middle Eastern Response.* Oxford: Oxford University Press, 2002.

Luft, Gal. "The Logic of Israel's Targeted Killing." *Middle East Quarterly* X, no. 1 (Winter 2003), 3–13.

Mahle, Melissa Boyle. *Denial and Deception: An Insider's View of the CIA from Iran-Contra to 9/11.* New York: Nation Books, 2004.

Maley, William, ed. *Fundamentalism Reborn?: Afghanistan and the Taliban.* New York: New York University Press, 1998.

Marsden, Peter. *The Taliban: War and Religion in Afghanistan.* New York: Zed Books, Ltd., 2002.

Marshall, Jonathan, Peter Dale Scott, and Jane Hunter. *The Iran-Contra Connection: Secret Teams and Covert Operations in the Reagan Era.* Boston, MA: South End Press, 1987.

McChrystal, Gen. Stanley A. "COMISAF's Initial Assessment (Kabul, Afghanistan, August 30, 2009)." *Washington Post,* September 21, 2009. http://www.washingtonpost.com/wp-dyn/content/article/2009/09/21/AR2009 092100110.html (accessed July 28, 2010).

Moynihan, Senator Daniel Patrick, and Senator Ron Wyden. "Secrecy in International and Domestic Policy Making: The Case for More Sunshine." *Federation of American Scientists,* October 2000. http://www.fas.org/sgp/library/wyden.html (accessed November 8, 2009).

National Commission on Terrorist Attacks Upon the United States. *The 9/11 Commission Report: Final Report of the National Commission on Terrorist Attacks Upon the United States.* New York: W. W. Norton & Co., 2004.

Niebuhr, Reinhold. *The Irony of American History.* Chicago, IL: The University of Chicago Press, 1952.

———. *Moral Man and Immoral Society: A Study in Ethics and Politics.* New York: Charles Schribner's Sons, 1934.

———. *The World Crisis and American Responsibility.* New York: Association Press, 1958.

Nojumi, Neamatollah. *The Rise of the Taliban in Afghanistan: Mass Mobilization, Civil War, and the Future of the Region.* New York: Palgrave, 2002.

Nye, Joseph S., Jr. *Soft Power: The Means to Success in World Politics.* New York: PublicAffairs, 2004.

Odysseos, Louiza, and Fabio Petito. *The International Political Thought of Carl Schmitt: Terror, Liberal War and the Crisis of Global Order.* London: Routledge, 2007.

O'Neill, Tip, and Gary Hymel. *All Politics Is Local and Other Rules of the Game.* New York: Times Books, 1994.

Orwell, George. *Dickens, Dali & Others: Studies in Popular Culture.* New York: Reynal & Hitchcock, 1946.

Pape, Robert A. *Dying to Win: The Strategic Logic of Suicide Terrorism.* New York: Random House, 2005.

———. "The Strategic Logic of Suicide Terrorism." *American Political Science Review,* August 2003: 343–361.

Piller, Paul R. *Terrorism and U.S. Foreign Policy.* Washington, DC: The Brookings Institution, 2001.

Powers, Thomas. *Intelligence Wars: American Secret History from Hitler to Al Qaeda.* New York: New York Review of Books, 2004.

Ul-Qadri, Muhammad Tahir. *Introduction to the Fatwa on Suicide Bombings and Terrorism.* Translated by Abdul Aziz Dabbagh (pending full translation).

Qutb, Sayyid. *Milestones.* 3rd ed. New Delhi, India: Markazi Maktaba Islami, 1991.

Rashid, Ahmed. *Taliban: Islam, Oil and the New Great Game in Central Asia.* London: I.B. Tauris & Co. Ltd., 2001.

Richelson, Jeffery T. *The U.S. Intelligence Community.* 4th ed. Cambridge, MA: Westview Press, 1999.

Ricks, Thomas E. *Fiasco: The American Adventure in Iraq, 2003–2005.* London: Penguin, 2007.

———. *The Gamble: General David Petreaus and the American Military Adventure in Iraq, 2006–2008.* London: Penguin, 2009.

Rohde, David. "Army Enlists Anthropology in War Zones." *The New York Times,* October 5, 2007. http://www.nytimes.com/2007/10/05/world/asia/05afghan.html (accessed November 1, 2009).

Roosevelt, Franklin D. "Fireside Chat: On the Declaration of War with Japan." Speech. Washington, DC, December 9, 1941.

Rothkopf, David J. *Running the World.* New York: PublicAffairs, 2004.

Roy, Olivier. *Afghanistan: From Holy War to Civil War.* Princeton, NJ: Darwin Press, 1995.

———. *The Failure of Political Islam.* Cambridge, MA: President and Fellows of Harvard College, 1994.

———. *Globalized Islam: The Search for a New Ummah.* New York: Columbia University Press, 2004.

———. *Islam and Resistance in Afghanistan.* 2nd ed. Cambridge, MA: Cambridge University Press, 1990.

———. *The Lessons of the Soviet/Afghan War.* London: International Institute for Strategic Studies, 1991.

———. *The Politics of Chaos in the Middle East.* New York: Columbia University Press, 2008.

———. *Secularism Confronts Islam.* Translated by George Holoch. New York: Columbia University Press, 2007.

Russell, Richard L. "CIA's Strategic Intelligence in Iraq." In *September 11, Terrorist Attacks, and U.S. Foreign Policy,* edited by Demetrios Caraley, 111–128. New York: The Academy of Political Science, 2002.

Ruthven, Malise. *Fundamentalism: The Search for Meaning.* Oxford, U.K.: Oxford University Press, 2004.

Sageman, Marc. *Leaderless Jihad: Terror Networks in the Twenty-First Century.* Philadelphia: University of Pennsylvania Press, 2007.

———. *Understanding Terror Networks.* Philadelphia: University of Pennsylvania Press, 2004.

Scahill, Jeremy. *Blackwater: The Rise of the World's Most Powerful Mercenary Army.* New York: Nation Books, 2007.

Scheuer, Michael. *Marching Toward Hell: America and Islam after Iraq.* New York: Free Press, 2008.

Schmitt, Carl. *The Concept of the Political.* Translated by George Schwab. Chicago, IL: University of Chicago Press, 1995.

———. *The Nomos of the Earth: In the International Law of the Jes Publicum Europaeum.* New York: Telos Press Publishing, 2003.

Shapiro, Jacob N., and C. Christine Fair. "Understanding Support for Islamist Militancy in Pakistan." *International Security* 34, no. 3 (Winter 2009/10): 79–118.

Sheehan, Neil. *A Bright Shining Lie: John Paul Vann and America in Vietnam.* New York: Random House, 2009.

Simpson, Gerry. *Law, War and Crime.* Cambridge: Polity Press, 2007.

Sloan, Stephen. *Beating International Terrorism: An Action Strategy for Preemption and Punishment.* Maxwell Air Force Base, AL: Air University Press, 2000.

Smith, Thomas W., Jr. *Encyclopedia of the Central Intelligence Agency.* New York: Facts on File, 2003.

Stern, Jessica. *Terror in the Name of God.* New York: HarperCollins Publishers, 2003.

———. *The Ultimate Terrorists.* Cambridge, MA: Harvard University Press, 1999.

Sun-Tzu. *The Art of War: Sun Zi's Military Methods.* Translated by Victor H. Mair. New York: Columbia University Press, 2007.

Theoharis, Athan. *The Quest for Absolute Security: The Failed Relations Among U.S. Intelligence Agencies.* New York: Ivan R. Dee, 2007.

Thucydides. *The History of the Peloponnesian War.* Edited by M. I. Finley. Translated by Rex Warner. New York: Penguin Books, 1954.

Trilling, Lionel. *The Liberal Imagination.* New York: New York Review of Books, 1978.

Troy, Thomas F. *Donovan and the CIA: A History of the Establishment of the Central Intelligence Agency.* Frederick, MD: University Publications of America, 1981.

———. *Wild Bill and Intrepid: Donovan, Stephenson, the Origins of CIA.* New Haven, CT: Yale University Press, 1996.

Tse-Tung, Mao. *On Guerrilla Warfare.* Translated by Samuel B. Griffith II. Champaign: University of Illinois Press, 1961.

Turk, Austin T. "Sociology of Terrorism." *Annual Review of Sociology* 30 (August 2004): 271–286.

Ullman, Lt. Gen. Harlan. *Unfinished Business: Afghanistan, the Middle East, and Beyond—Defusing the Dangers that Threaten America's Security.* New York: Citadel Press, 2003.

U.S. Army and Marine Corps. *The Army/Marine Corps Counterinsurgency Field Manual.* Chicago, IL: The University of Chicago Press, 2007.

Vogel, Frank E. *Islamic Law and Legal System: Studies of Saudi Arabia.* Leiden, Netherlands: Studies in Islamic Law and Society, Koninklijke Brill NV, 2000.

Watts, Michael J. "Revolutionary Islam: A Geography of Modern Terror." In *Violent Geographies: Fear, Terror, and Political Violence,* edited by Allan Pred and Derek Gregory, 175–204. New York: Routledge, 2007.

Weaver, Mary Anne. "Inventing Al-Zarqawi." *The Atlantic Monthly,* July/August 2006, 86–100.

Weber, Ralph E., ed. *Spymasters: Ten CIA Officers in their Own Words.* Wilmington, DE: Scholarly Resources Inc., 1999.

Weiner, Tim. *Legacy of Ashes: The History of the CIA.* New York: Anchor Books, 2008.

Weizman, Eyal. *Hollow Land: Israel's Architecture of Occupation.* London and New York: Verso, 2007.

Westbrook, David A. *City of Gold: An Apology for Global Capitalism in a Time of Discontent.* New York: Routledge, 2004.

———. "The Globalization of American Law," *Theory, Culture and Society, Special Issue on Problematizing Global Knowledge* 23: 526–528.

———. "Islamic International Law and Public International Law: Separate Expressions of World Order." *Virginia Journal of International Law* 33 (1993): 819.

———. "Keynote Address: Theorizing the Diffusion of Law: Conceptual Difficulties, Unstable Imaginations, and the Effort to Think Gracefully Nonetheless." *International Law Journal Symposium: The Diffusion of Law in the 21st Century.* Harvard Law School, Cambridge, MA: Harvard International Law Journal, 2006. 489–506.

———. "Law Through War." *Buffalo Law Review* 48 (2000): 299–348.

———. *Navigators of the Contemporary: Why Ethnography Matters.* Chicago, IL: The University of Chicago Press, 2008.

———. "Strategic Consequences of Radical Islamic Neofundamentalism." *ORBIS* 51, no. 3 (Summer 2007): 461–477.

Whelan, Richard. *Al-Qaedaism: The Threat to Islam, the Threat to the World.* Dublin: Ashfield Press, 2005.

Wright, Donald P., and Timothy R. Reese, with the Contemporary Operations Study Team. *On Point II: Transition to the New Campaign: The United States Army in Operation IRAQI FREEDOM May 2003–January 2005.* Fort Leavenworth, KS: Combat Studies Institute Press, US Army Combined Arms Center, 2008.

Zahab, Mariam Abou, and Olivier Roy. *Islamist Networks: The Afghan-Pakistan Connection.* New York: Columbia University Press, 2004.

Zakaria, Fareed. *The Post-American War.* New York: W. W. Norton & Co., 2009.

INDEX

ABOUT THE AUTHOR

David A. Westbrook is Floyd H. & Hilda L. Hurst Faculty Scholar and Professor of Law at the University at Buffalo, the State University of New York. Westbrook writes about the social and intellectual consequences of contemporary political economy. His work influences numerous disciplines, including law, economics, finance, sociology, anthropology, cultural studies, and design. He has spoken worldwide to academics, business and financial leaders, members of the security community, civil institutions, and governments. Westbrook's most recent book is *Out of Crisis: Rethinking Our Financial Markets* (Paradigm 2009).